WEAR IT PROUDLY

Wear It Proudly

LETTERS BY

William Shinji Tsuchida

UNIVERSITY OF CALIFORNIA PRESS
Berkeley and Los Angeles · 1947

UNIVERSITY OF CALIFORNIA PRESS
BERKELEY AND LOS ANGELES
CALIFORNIA

◇

CAMBRIDGE UNIVERSITY PRESS
LONDON, ENGLAND

COPYRIGHT, 1947, BY
THE REGENTS OF THE UNIVERSITY OF CALIFORNIA

FOREWORD

When a regular infantry unit receives a presidential citation for "outstanding performance of duty in action against the enemy," it is pretty well known that the unit has suffered heavy casualties—usually more than one hundred per cent. Any survivor would necessarily have a rather stirring story to tell—if he could put it into words,—particularly if he were a front-line aid man, whose hands were perforce in the blood that was being spilled, right at the moment when bleeding was most severe.

Company I of the 71st Infantry was just such a unit; and fortunately, one of its medics, the aid man with the second platoon, wrote exceptionally good letters about the action of his unit as it fought its way across southern France and into the Austrian Alps. With no other background than this, his letters and the story they tell would make an absorbing narrative. But this man's own background makes his story especially significant. He was Japanese. At least, that's what his mirror told him. Heredity decreed it, and he was the last man to object—he and the other two Japanese who served in the 44th Division.

But he was American, too. We know, and we have been told if we didn't know it before, that man is what he experiences; his mind is the sum of what his eyes have seen and what his physical senses have told him

FOREWORD

was so. There is no need to be too literal about man's mind here. It need only be pointed out that this man's experience was American, totally American: on the Monday after Pearl Harbor he was in a U. S. Army recruiting office in San Francisco.

Will Tsuchida fought with the Seventh Army. His letters pick up the story a few days after he rode an LCI into a blasted but peaceful harbor in France. Anyone who was in charge of censorship for an infantry battalion can now be amused by the amount of detail in Tsuchida's letters, and can understand as well why a few hiatuses were cut in here and there. By and large, however, he left out tactical details, description of weapons, unit designations, and statistics on casualties, which is what censorship primarily required him to do. The letters thus do not reveal, unless studied carefully in their relation to documents declassified since the war, very much about the military aspect of his war. It doesn't matter. His was a real and personal part of the experience of every front-line medic. His specific description rings true, whether of the smell of cordite in an area on the receiving end of an enemy barrage, the cold feeling in his stomach during an attack, the high regard for the combat friends he carried in and sweated out, or the young man's tears—he was twenty-three—that couldn't be held when eventually he was separated from the outfit. His letters deal not with counters, but with coins. He took no great pains to polish them; he did not need to. He was naturally felicitous, and painstaking

FOREWORD

editing could only rob his letters of their immediacy; any combat infantryman will attest that nothing artificial has been added to their flavor. Nothing need be.

For one thing, these letters were not written with a publisher in mind. If Will Tsuchida were to write a preface for this little book, it would surely start out, "This isn't my idea." He could hardly more than gasp when he found out that they were all typed in manuscript form and in the hands of the University of California Press. He had only suspected that something was up—something unusual. Several friends, including Gordon McKenzie and Paul Taylor, of the University faculty, had casually mentioned how much they liked his letters. He didn't remember having written to these friends, but dismissed the matter. When his brother, to whom most of these overseas letters had been addressed, slipped a power of attorney under his pen and said, "Here, sign this; it's a good deal," Will just signed, not knowing that in so doing he had given legal authority to a one-man steering committee, bent on bringing these letters to some prominence. Will's attitude is best epitomized in his good-natured remark, "Those pictures of me will have to come out. If you put any people in, it ought to be just the men in the platoon."

A certain documentary importance lies in these letters so far as they reveal the feelings of a Japanese American who is homesick without a home, who is fighting for his country, and fighting well, without knowing that his country will restore to him and to his family

FOREWORD

even their few possessions and that little respect which it held for them before he went to war. The cynic may say that he, and the other Japanese Americans, had no choice. No cynic, however, could base such a claim on any knowledge of infantry combat and its opportunities for the malingerer.

So far as the spirit and deed of another can be assessed through his spontaneous writings, it can be said that Will Tsuchida was of a piece with the fabric of the wartime G.I.; he was a regular G.I., and one of the best. So far as one man can symbolize his kind, he contributes to the understanding of his race of Americans. Let no man who values his prejudices bring them with him as he reads Tsuchida's mail. They won't survive the reading.

DAVID R. BROWER,
A former Combat Infantryman, serving with the 10th Mountain Division

March 25, 1947

THE LETTERS

France, 22 Sept. 1944

Dear Hime and Eiichi,

Well we're living in the woods again and you know how I feel about that. It's the same old story—those awful cold damp nights and living out of an inverted helmet. As I said before, it's the little things that bother us more than the major fact that we are supposed to be fighting a war. When this war is over I'm going to have steak every day, a fur-lined toilet, breakfast in bed, automatic showers, and not to forget, my own personal laundry system. Speaking of the laundry, I have stuff piled up from the boat ride. We wash whenever we can in our helmets and if we are near a creek.

Now something of more interest to you—France and the people. The hedgerows are a nuisance to military maneuvers and our stray baseballs. There are no fences in France and no doubt the hedgerows have determined the property boundaries for centuries. They are a combination of thorns, tangleweed, brush, and trees—in short, a mess to go through. The rest of the country is very green, heavy with foliage and kind of pretty with the little hills and knolls. The houses are stone (just like the pictures) and invariably with shellholes and broken windows. The cows wander around on the loose giving the whole thing a pastoral scene (and also leaving behind their contributions to the bivouac area). Lots of apple trees with green apples so we made some apple sauce in a bucket in a last attempt of desperation to satisfy our hunger. The people ride around in two-wheeled horse carts or bicycles. They wear berets, T-shirts, and nondescript G.I. clothes. They have wooden shoes or G.I. shoes. Even the little kids plop around with big G.I. shoes. It doesn't take long to realize that they have been hard hit and are hard up. I can't bitch too much about my food because they have even less. We are supposed to treat the civilian's medical needs (we would anyway—after you see all the open sores on the kids). Just about all the civilians are suffering from malnutrition which causes sores on their bodies. None of the adults have asked for any medical aid but we have been patching up a lot of kids. The kids are of course skinny and seem small.

I wish I could tell you some of the towns we went through because it wasn't very long ago that their names were in all the papers. These small provincial towns are colorful too. The buildings are stone and are built next to each other. The streets are cobblestone and there's always a square (but it's round) in the center of town.

No neon signs of course and I'm glad there aren't because they wouldn't fit into the picture anyway. The natives say that there was heavy street fighting and I can believe it because there is evidence of it.

In your letters will you tell me what is censored out (to the best of your knowledge) so I won't make the same mistake twice?

You mentioned that maybe you should send me packages every two or three weeks so they won't pile up on me. Hell no! Send one every day if you like because we can sure take care of it. No PX's out here so we are starved for candy, nuts and other good eats. Whatever you do don't send canned meat like Spam. They feed us so much of that stuff it's coming out of my ears. Lots of cigarettes for the guys (1 pack a day) furnished by the army.

Please send me some of those fancy candy bars as you did once before. And remember that lots of small packages are better than one big one. Wrap everything in waterproof wrapping (like bread wrappings). I have enough pipe tobacco now. Oh yes, please put one candlestick in the next package (not over 12 inches long). I will ask you for candles from time to time. Try to find nice fat ones or the kind they used to have in sporting goods stores with the wax in a small tin cup (I doubt if they have any more of those).

The following stuff is not urgent but if you should happen to run across any please send them. A good map of France with all the names of little towns on it. If they are expensive forget it. You asked what I would like for Christmas. Well I wonder if you could get a (white) sweatshirt with U.C. or a bear on it. My size is 38. If you can get one please do this for me. Write in with indelible ink on the inside of the collar "T-5699" with about ½-inch letters. That's my clothes mark. And, I am still on the lookout for the ideal stationery holder. They are made of leather with zipper and look like a small school binder.

I have enclosed dix francs which are worth 20 cents (2 cents = 1 franc). We will be paid in francs from now on but there is still nothing to buy so I will probably exchange it for U.S. money orders.

I will write a shorter letter to the folks so be sure to tell them everything I told you. I am feeling fine (just starved a little) and will take care of myself. So long for now,

SHINJI

Keep writing!

P.S. Yes, please send the snapshots from Wisconsin.

France, 26 Sept. 1944

Dear H and E,

Still going strong and feeling all right. Even had a USO show come up here to "entertain" us. Personally I wish they gave their space to some cases of cokes. It was an old vaudeville act and only the old-timers from N.Y. got a kick out of it. And then we had a Red Cross Clubmobile come by with coffee and do-nuts. If the enlisted men tried to talk to the girls the officers would give them something equivalent to a "scram buddy" and take over like big operators. And so that's the way it was, a bunch of EM's standing around with mouths open watching the conversation go back and forth between the RC girls and the officers. Like watching a tennis match. But that's the way it always is—do you think we could get near these movie actresses? Hell no, it's always the officers mess or club that they see. Oh well, as we always end arguments of this type, "When the war is over———."

Speaking of chicken spit, it goes with the army regardless of where it is. They go as far as fining for not saluting or being out of uniform around here. Here's the difference in civilian life. If you get cold you put on more clothing and if you're hot you remove it, right? Well in the army you try something like that and you get hell for being out of uniform. Probably a reason for it but I'm sure I can't see it. Just adds to the misery.

Good news. We had fresh meat yesterday—pork

chops. And Sunkist oranges today. That's more like it. We had so much C-ration that we were beginning to look like the cans.

Please remember that as long as I'm "bitching" about the army and the food and other trivial stuff, you don't have to worry because it's a sign that things are normal and that I am in no danger. I guess that's about all I can say.

Mail from the states has taken a back seat to supplies and for that reason we haven't got any mail that you have written meant for overseas. The last letter I got from you sounded as if you thought I was still on the East Coast. I bet that letter came over on the same boat with me. I'm still looking for that package with the nuts and candy which was meant for me at Phillips. We couldn't receive packages at our staging area so I have no idea where it is now. And boy could we use it now!

Enclosed is a 25 dollar money order. It must be troublesome for you to always keep sending and getting my money but I never know what kind of a situation we're going to be in. And right now there is absolutely nothing to spend it on and I don't want to keep it on me. So for now—"à plus tard,"

SHINJI

31 September 1944

Dear H and E,

You've heard of those wartime coincidences. Well I have one to tell now. When I left Intelligence School in Minnesota I went to the U. of Nebraska with a fellow called Vernon. (There's a picture of him in my album with Kathleen.) We got to be pretty good friends. He was a Med student but all the ASTP Med schools were full so he took languages. He almost talked me into going with him (and I almost did) but I was going to be an engineer or bust. So he went to Harvard and I went to Missouri. After the AST bust I lost track of him and I figured he went to another school. But far from it. The other day we were hiking along when all of a sudden I saw him come out of a driveway in the hedgerow carrying a water can. I couldn't stop then so we yelled at each other and I found out what outfit he was in. So that night I got permission from my sergeant and went back to the place I saw him. He had about the same story as I did and was busted to a private. As usual the army screwed up. He's a medical student and they make him a rifleman, and I get in the medics. Jeez! We are in the same army but he is in another division. What a classification system! Well it was good to see him anyway. C'est tout,

SHINJI

1 Oct. 1944

Dear H and E,

Am writing this after dark so don't blame me for any strange figures. I just wanted to let you know that our mail finally caught up with us yesterday and it was good to hear from you again (from Aug. 30 to Sept. 21 inclusive). Let me know how you have been getting my mail. I hope not like the way we have(n't) been getting it. But still no packages! Candy right now is worth its weight in gold. The fellows trade two and three packs of cigarettes for a one-cent bar of Hershey!

Feeling fine (as much as can be expected) and the food is getting better. Weather is cold and wet. And still don't know where we will end up. Will write again,

SHINJI

LETTERS BY TSUCHIDA

9 Oct. 1944

Dear H and E,

Thanks for always writing, it means a lot and I can't thank you enough. Especially now when it rains every day and the wind blows like mad. Everything is wet and oozy with mud.

I didn't send you that copy of "Yank" with the article about the 100th Infantry because I knew you would get a copy from Helen. But don't you think it's a good magazine. We think it's tops. They even tell the officers to go to hell sometimes.

You are right about wet feet. It's known as "trench foot" or technically as "immersion foot." You know what that means. Those poor line company guys had to stand in their holes so long that their blood finally stagnated in their feet. Every one of those guys deserves a medal (but they won't get it I bet). Anyway we have been getting lots of instructions on its prevention. Until a few days ago, we couldn't have fires of any kind but the company CO's complained finally about the wet feet of their men so now we can dry them over the fires.

I'm sorry you have a tough time shopping for me but just send me anything that can be eaten easily (no preparation). And keep the candy, cookies, nuts coming. Make it a rule to have something to eat in every package. So long for now,

SHINJI

10 Oct. 1944

Dear H and E,

Got another V-mail from you today (Sept. 22) Thanks again. Eiichi, you can wear anything of mine if it fits. You bet I'm going to buy a new outfit. It will be a lot of sport suits and jackets.

That city you mentioned in your letter—we won't get to see it during the duration because first, it's off limits subject to court martial, and second, we are not near it, and third, what the heck makes you think we have time for sight seeing. But as you say I can hope, and I do hope that I will get to see it since I'm over here, but not right now!

How is your house hunting coming along? I wish you the best of luck in finding it, and hope that it will have a kitchenette capable of taking care of me when I come home. Do they trouble you any with prejudice and that sort of thing? Excuse me for asking questions with obvious answers but I would like to know if they give you a tough time. So long for now,

SHINJI

12 Oct. 1944

Dear H and E,

Still raining in France and it is plenty muddy. It is a messy job to break down and pack equipment in the rain. Shades of Louisiana—only no umpire with white flags this time.

Say folks, please do me a favor. What it amounts to is that I want you to listen to the news broadcasts of the war in this neck of the woods and tell me what you hear. As is usually the case, outsiders know what's going on better than we. We want to know what they mention about us if we are mentioned at all. I don't mean a complete news report but be sure to let us know if they should ever mention us. Walter Winchell is supposed to have criticized this division several times so I bet he was surprised we came over.

I wrote to mom for some powdered Nestle's chocolate and for some powdered soup like bouillon, chicken broth, etc. Please tell her to make sure the chocolate is sweetened with sugar already and that soups are complete and can be easily made with the addition of hot water only. Would you kind of supervise it and see that she doesn't buy too big of a package of the stuff, and that if possible she wraps it in some waterproofing.

Also send me (this letter is more of a requisition slip) my leather gloves. If you can't find them please buy me a pair suitable for heavy duty with lots of fleece lining.

Also, I broke the lens to my glasses (left side only). No hurry but when you get one ordered please put it in with a box of eats. Feeling O.K. so far, slight cold.

SHINJI

P.S. Please send a box of eats, candy nuts cookies etc.

23 Oct. 1944

Dear H and E,

Just to let you know that I am perfectly all right before you start to worry why I haven't written. This is it, or some phrase like that. We are really in it now. I am writing from the kitchen of an old French house that is half caved in, with our aid station in the front room. The wounded are coming in and boy it is really something awful. We have to duck every so often on account of the shelling. I sure will have lots of stories to tell you after this. We treated a German officer who had a wound in his thigh. The prisoners are going by in small groups. I will write to the folks at the first chance so in the meantime please phone them. I am in perfect health so don't worry. Just keep writing. So long for now,

SHINJI

France, 23 Oct. 1944

Dear H and E,

Hello again while I have a chance to write. We are being relieved today for a few hours and it sure is good to lie down for a while. The other day we were supposed to have our first rest period but we were called back. From that you can surmise to what degree we are having casualties since I can't tell you that directly. Anyway we got as far as the showers and I had my first shower in about two months. You should see us now. We are caked with mud from head to toe and my clothes are ready to be peeled off of me. My underclothes are oily black and I sure would like to change. The shower point is about 20 minutes away. No ducking, no shrapnel. Like everything else in the army we got in a long line for the showers and when we finally got under the water we had only five minutes. I guess that was about the most enjoyable five minutes in my life. And after that we had to come back here regretfully.

I am feeling all right and I don't have a scratch on me so please don't worry. I can trust you to tell the folks just the right things. I do have trouble with my stomach and French water however. Maybe it's the lousy rations. I have had stomach-aches several times and that sure gets me down. Which brings up the topic of food. It's all K-rations and dog biscuits, all cold.

Right now I am at the advance aid station which is relatively safe compared with the front lines but we still get hit several times a day. We are in an old French building that used to be a bar at one time because the fountains and cocktail glasses are still intact. And since the civilians were evacuated and since the chickens are still around, you know the inevitable—stewed chickens.

What a mess this whole business is. My mind is one confused conglomeration of incidents, the basic fears of night, and the waiting for daylight. The rest of it I would just as soon forget because it is so rotten. I hope everybody with the soft war jobs realizes the horrible days and nights the line company men have to spend out here. It's really awful that these young kids have to go through this sort of thing. I don't feel very much like telling my stories yet so I will tell them to you some other time. And the other thing that gets me down is the BS artists back at the main aid station who don't have to risk their necks every time they go out, yet they brag the most. Will I be glad to go home!

Got your letters regularly, with the pictures. Thanks, and keep it up. Please send me small cans or jars of jellies, preserves. Our diet lacks vegetables so send small cans of tomato juice, soups, fruit. And be sure to make the packages in a variety, not just one item in one box. Particular ain't I but we don't have barracks bags any more to keep stuff in. Just what we can get in our pockets. So mix candy, cookies, fruits. No, I hate coffee and never want to see it again and the French don't drink it so don't send it. So long for now,

SHINJI

France, 27 Oct. 1944

Dear Eiichi,

Now don't get excited because it doesn't amount to much. I was told today that I would get the Purple Heart. Here is the dope. Yesterday I got caught by two mortar shells, the first one cut up my thumb right near the base and by the time I turned around the second one kicked my back near the right shoulder and also my right elbow. Now all these places are only scratches and I have been cut worse by opening tin cans. But the main thing is that I was plenty lucky that it was only scratches. In fact I have been very lucky so far because I have been knocked down by bigger and closer blasts and the shrapnel always seemed to miss me. Oh yes, the shrapnel that hit my elbow stuck to my flesh and the doctor picked it out and gave it to me so I will keep it for a souvenir, hoping that they won't come any bigger. The fact that I shed blood allows me the Purple Heart and that's all there is to that.

The irony of it all is that men are dying for the same medal and here I get a few scratches. About the only thing I can see in it with a fair conscience is that it may give me some extra points in mustering out.

So that's the whole story. It only took a few minutes to patch me up and I am now back at work. But please don't play it up because the men are dying for the same thing right now. I was very lucky. Will write again,

SHINJI

France, 28 Oct. 1944

Dear H and E,

I got your V-mail letters of the 11th, 12th and air mail of 17th of October today. Let me tell you it is good to read something that has no connection with the confusion here. I get in such a daze sometimes that I force myself to read something when I can, like a magazine or an old letter. What it amounts to is you wonder whether you should eat now or later and hope you have a dry place to sleep tonight and hope that the casualties will slow down. Everything is hope, hope.

This may be censored but since you are so insistent on asking me about Paris I will stick my neck out and say that I saw the Eiffel Tower but it was far from a pleasant experience. The truth is I was soaked to the skin, dirty, tired, cramped, and just sick of anything connected with France. Nope, if I'm going to see Paree I want to do it proper and when that time comes I will get all the souvenirs you want. You bet.

I will try to answer some of your questions now. Yes I think John's outfit is in France now because I saw a picture in the Stars and Stripes just today of some of their men. As usual their captions still call us Japs or Jap-Americans. Gee it sure will be the day when they quit hyphenating and leave off the first part.

I'm glad to hear you're taking up golf, Hime. You bet it's a date some nice peaceful afternoon. I hope you can teach me by then.

As for your other question it requires a specific answer so I can't tell you that. We can mention things in general but never specifically.

Remember when I mentioned in my last letter how we had trouble with the guys in the aid station. It's a funny thing but some guys just won't go all the way when it comes to a little sacrifice, especially when there are guys dying all around us. Well we have two drivers in our detachment who are supposed to help us evacuate the wounded from the lines by driving their jeeps as close as possible to the front lines. When we go into the woods to evacuate a casualty they are supposed to be waiting for us until we come back so they can rush to the aid station with the casualty. If they are not there it means we have to take them in on our backs on the litters to the aid station. And that has happened several times and it also means hours of backbreaking work especially in this terrain. A jeep can do it in a few minutes with chains on the tires. But most important of all it can mean a life saved. For instance yesterday, we went deep into the woods and got a fellow with chest wounds. He had been lying there for about twelve hours unattended because the Germans snipe at the medics and mostly because artillery was so heavy you couldn't show your fingernails without getting shrapnel. He had lost a lot of blood and I couldn't feel any pulse. His color was very pale. It took us a full hour to get him out of there to the clearing. We were so exhausted we could hardly stand up. Well, we expected the jeep to be there waiting but our hearts sank a foot when we didn't see any vehicle in sight. So we had to take our casualty in on foot. He was still conscious when we finally got him in another two hours later. The aid station gave him plasma and boy we all sighed a thanks to some mythical God when the kid opened his lips to speak. Oh yes, the drivers—both of them were taking it easy smoking. They claimed it was too dangerous at the advance collecting point for them. Boy we blew our top and the Lt. bawled the daylights out of them. I think we are going to have new drivers.

I don't know why I chose that particular story but I am just writing what comes to my mind now. I have so many confused incidents in my mind of worse spots that I have been in that I will write them to you if I feel like it.

Today I am getting a rest because my shoulder is still a little sore from that mortar shrapnel. I don't deserve this rest because my buddies are still out there evacuating the wounded and compared to the line men I have it relatively easy.

I will write again. Tell me more about that little town you visited. It sounds good. No packages yet. So long for now,

SHINJI

France, 29 Oct. 1944, Sunday

Dear H and E,

Just a quickie to let you know I am all right. Today we got all our rations together and put them in one pot and added potatoes and onions from the field here. Also, the Chaplain, who works with us now, caught and cooked two chickens. We set plates on the table from this French house and sat down for a meal. The Chaplain said grace and it was enough to put a lump in your throat. But what a meal that was, and hot coffee too. We were being shelled all this time but that couldn't keep us from our meals. One shell shook cinders into our coffee but nobody cared. What a life!

I got your V-mail of the 9th of Oct. So long for now,

SHINJI

P.S. Please send a box of eats.

30 Oct. 1944, Halloween

Dear H and E,

Tonight is Halloween night back home and the boys were talking about it. We are gathered around a candle in the center of the table and reading and writing letters. Outside and upstairs the shells are landing and shaking the building. We are safe down here in the cellar from anything but a direct hit. So we sit here and are appreciating the rest. But we can hear the line men up there firing away with their small arms, which means the Germans are trying to infiltrate, as they do as soon as night falls. Boy, all the praise in the world is not half enough for the infantrymen who have to sweat every minute they are in the line.

It's also Kiyoko's birthday tomorrow isn't it? Well I forgot to write her so please tell her the next time you see her that I remembered. Also Bess and George's anniversary.

I am sending the Purple Heart medal home to you. Do what you like with it—maybe the folks would like to keep it. It is really very pretty, but you can have 'em all. Boy, all I can say is that I am very lucky. I will keep the ribbon in case we ever wear blouses again. As the boys say, "It's good for a few drinks." I'm only kidding. Here's the funny thing. I am a medic working with one battalion and when I get hit I go to the medics of another outfit. It just happened to be closer, their aid station. But in the rush of patching me up they overlooked my leg. So when I got back to my own aid station I discovered a small cut just below my left knee cap. Lucky again.

Thanks for sending the pictures of Glen Gray I got in today's mail. They came out pretty good don't you think?

Oh my god! Do you mean to say Kiyoko is sending me Spam? and beans? Straighten her out, will you? Although I appreciate everybody's sending me things I think you better supervise or coach them. Another thing on the nix list is chocolate bars. The army's idea of candy ration is penny Hershey bars. It's better than nothing but it's enough to make you pull your hair out. Well good night,

SHINJI

France, 2 Nov. 1944

Dear H and E,

Enclosing a $52.00 money order. Please use it if you like or invest it for me in any way you like. I guess bonds are the best. There hasn't been anything I could spend money on for the past few months so there is no sense in losing it in some muddy foxhole.

It didn't cost anything to send the medal home. The government pays for it.

The chaplain and his assistant travel with us now as I told you before. Well the chaplain's assistant, whose name is "Smitty," carries a small organ around with him. The instrument is about four by four by three and is pedal operated. They can afford to carry it around with them because they have a vehicle of their own. Well, a few days ago Smitty uncrated the organ and tonight we are giving it its debut. And what a scene it makes. Shells are going off all around the building shaking the hell out of us but we are more intent in yelling requests into Smitty's ear. The French family seems amazed at the American army's equipment. Now Smitty is playing some polkas and the "Emperor's Waltz" so the boys can dance with the two daughters. The old lady is laughing her head off because we have our two comedians dancing with them. It sure is good to see them laugh.

I don't think I ever told you about the family. There is papa, mama, Margo who is 26, Marie who is 16, and a bunch of little kids. When we moved in they were peeved at everything and the war because just as soon as they got rid of the Germans we moved in in the same manner. There just wasn't time for a formal request. We needed an aid station quick and their house, what's left of it, served the purpose. So we didn't exactly feel like liberators. But now they have noticed the difference in our manners from the "Boches" as they call them, and we have arrived at a mutual confidence in each other. We trade rations for eggs, chickens, bread. Marie is really a knockout, brunette with dark eyes and resembles Maureen O'Hara and of course she takes a lot of kidding from the boys. Margo is the thoughtful one. Her husband has been in a German prison camp since the fall of France, to the best of her knowledge. The uncertainty must be hell on her; we see her crying often. She has been a great help in the aid station. She cooks hot soup, coffee for casualties, cooks and cleans up for us. Once I came back from the lines covered from head to toe with mud and soaked to the skin. She looked at me and said, "Mon dieu, mon pauvre petit!" Then she did something which I will never forget. She led me to the fire and on her knees she scraped the mud off of my pants with a paring knife, like the humble servant. Who says this isn't the little people's war?

We sleep in the cellar with the whole family and boy what a crowd! I can remember the little kids crying for the urinal can in the dark and if we weren't so tired we would laugh.

Now this fellow Smitty can really play. He also went to AST, and used to play at Radio City. As usual, like anybody who knows anything about music he knows what's good. He had classical training but he knows Duke, Louis, and he knows everybody down at "Nick's" in Greenwich Village. It sure is good to hear something strictly from home. Singing is spontaneous with the old nostalgic tunes like "I'm in the Mood for Love," "Thanks for the Memories," and best of all is "White Christmas."

Now he's playing all the orchestra theme songs. He knows "Let's Dance" and "Goodbye" complete with Benny's clary parts.

I guess I can tell you we were relieved today for a few days. So for a few days we will be in reserve. That accounts for all the time I have for letters today.

My shoulder is O.K. now because it's starting to "scab" over now so please do not worry.

Please send a box of eats! So long for now,

SHINJI

P.S. Smitty is now playing the entire score to "Porgy and Bess," and he really knows it but everybody is making too much noise, not to mention the shelling.

France, 5 Nov. 1944, Sunday

Dear H and E,

Today is Sunday and believe it or not we had services in spite of the war going on very near us. Smitty set up his organ in the barn next to the aid station and you would be surprised how in your mind you can wander off thousands of miles to a place called home by just singing a few hymns. Everybody had that look in his eyes. And we really want to go home now!

Take last night for instance. Smitty was playing a lot of themes for us, any symphony we would name. The guy is remarkable and he must have had a terrific training. We got around to Beethoven and even without complete orchestration his stuff is really on the ball. As Smitty says, it's the subtlety in it that gives you those pleasant chills up your spine. And continuing, the trouble with the Romanticist period, was the obviousness of their themes. Take Peter T's melodies. Pretty and all but sort of shallow next to Beethoven. Then I told Smitty that when we run into something like that in jazz we try to separate the forms because of the danger of criticizing the form and not the actual music. To which he replied he never realized that and that I was right, but I think he was just being polite because he is too good a musician not to know anything that I can even surmise. Which brings me up to Louis. Louis' stuff was always (nearly) subtle, which may account for its being interesting in the effect it had.

Back to the war. (Thanks to Smitty for his wonderful therapy against battle jitters even if it is momentary.) I'm writing by candlelight and sometimes the concussions from the shells going off are so strong that the flame goes out from the sound waves (plus actual pressure). You wonder how such terrific sound can be created, which alone is enough to break a man down, minus the shrapnel.

I found out another thing. The field artillery is really a racket compared to the infantry. I met some of my friends from AST who are in FA and they are so far behind the lines that they do not act as if there was a war going on. And they get about one casualty to our hundred if that many.

I am feeling fine and am enjoying this break as much as possible. But it's colder than heck. I hope everybody can last this winter in good health because I notice more fellows coughing and blowing noses. Also diarrhea among the men from lousy eating conditions. But out here they can be considered the least of our troubles.

SHINJI

9 Nov. 1944, France

Dear H and E,

I'm writing this only because you enclosed the envelope in your letter, which is a very good idea. Also a good policy is to write whenever I can and this is no desk I'm writing on either. A ration box to be exact.

Our first snow fell today and it only brings out our hopes for an early victory all the more. We also saw the snow-capped mountains today and instead of looking beautiful (which they are) they only fill us with the dread of a tough fight ahead. If only it were summer we were looking forward to rather than winter.

[Censored]

Meanwhile our "glamour boys" (that's what we call the air corps) are going over on great bomber raids every day and there are enough planes in the sky to walk on. We often wonder why a sight like that doesn't depress the German soldier into surrendering. And "wham!" goes a German shell.

Feeling O.K. except for my cold. Please send me cheap handkerchiefs that I can throw away.

SHINJI

LETTERS BY TSUCHIDA

Nov. 15, 1944

Dear H and E,

I hate to mention the war every time I write but it is really here laid out before our very eyes so please excuse me. I don't want to be the alarmist but I think you would rather have me tell you the real dope rather than beat around the bush. I always tell mom and pop that I am sleeping in buildings and everything is fine.

As I have said before, please don't worry if there is a lapse in my correspondence. Just figure that we are, shall we say, "busy." I have been getting your letters regularly and I'm glad to read them and the relative innocence that people back home have of the hell out here. I don't think you will believe some of the things veterans will tell you after this war because there are no equivalent experiences in horror and suffering to compare with outside of war.

Thanks for the University of Chicago bulletin. Yes, please send me more although it gripes me to read one in the middle of a shelling. Just send me home.

The weather is bad. The mud oozes and the sleet cuts like a knife and the snow puts a false blanket over everything. My heart sinks a foot when I get to a wounded man covered with an inch of snow. You can just imagine the suffering they go through before medical aid can get to them. Boy the real heroes are these line company guys. I'll never forget some of them for their guts.

You asked in your letters where I sleep. This might shed a little light. Night before last it was too dark to dig in so Warren and I went over to a German half track, removed the dead driver, threw out the junk, carefully remembering the booby traps, found a grenade under the seat and removed that, and then climbed in and huddled together to shiver the night out. It was a mansion compared to a water-filled hole.

No packages yet but some of the guys have been getting some in wet, soggy shape. Please wrap everything in waterproof stuff because the mail bags have to lie out in rain in some port area for weeks before transportation is available. I am feeling O.K. and will take care of myself.

SHINJI

P.S. Please send a cheap fountain pen, box of eats.

21 Nov. 1944, France

Dear H and E,

My silence for the past few days will have to speak for how busy we have been. Every minute has been exciting if that is the word for it. I think my appetite for excitement has been cured, especially when it involves bloodshed and losing good friends and the miserable backbreaking work with the infantry. I am so homesick now that it is only when we are active that we can forget it.

We haven't been getting mail or packages for the past few days. Transportation must be a hell of a problem. Once again I would like to warn you to wrap everything solid and waterproof. The boys are getting packages in terrible condition and it's really a shame. Don't forget I still like things like popcorn, potato chips, cellophane bag candies, so please include them in a package too. Some more on the nix list are canned meats and cheese and Hershey bars (which means these things are definitely G.I.). Yes I know that I am very choosy but these delicacies could make me very happy.

We sure have an interesting setup today. The town we are in now was taken this morning and it is the biggest one we have taken yet. So it's what you might call still hot and little by little they are rounding up the snipers left behind. We are really in Swastika land now. Storm troopers, Gestapo headquarters, Heil Hitler salutes, huge swastika banners that drape from balconies—these are real things now. In fact the troops came in so fast they didn't have time to hide or take these things with them when they retreated. Another difference is the kids. Back in Normandy they would come out and cheer us with V-finger signs and all. This changes the closer we get to Germany. The civilians still watch us from their doorways, probably with doubt, and wait for us to "break the ice." And it is an opinion shared by most of us that they are just as much German as they are French. I have noticed that the German accent dominates the French. So there you are. Do you suppose it makes much difference to them which side of the line they are on? Anyway, to the average American foot soldier who watches his buddies die and dig for his life on this lousy French soil these little things make him ask "Why the hell don't the French fight their own wars?" It's a small viewpoint but you get that way when you run out of strength and expect principles to take you over these hills.

So now I'm sitting in a building which the Germans used as a hospital before they left. Every room, and this is the absolute truth, has (or rather had) a picture of Adolf in expensive looking frames. Don't worry, I didn't forget to represent the Tsuchida family by shoving my foot through that mustached face. And of course there are the hundreds of typical Nazi slogans all over the walls. I am enclosing the one that was on the front door of this building which says "You are a German! The salute in here is Heil Hitler." All the clocks are still running and on time. This is German paper which we found here by the reams. Also several German typewriters are now tapping away letters. Telephones in every room, good desk lamps, venetian blinds, we got the works this time.

Your letter from your friend of the "Y" was very good and I only wish I had his advice earlier. Incidentally, we found leaflets on the line which were a part of German propaganda to their soldiers saying that since Roosevelt won the election again the U.S. was bound to lose the war now. That's how we found out Roosevelt won again, plus a rare copy of the Stars and Stripes, which is usually late anyway.

My health is O.K. and my cold is not so bad now. Stomach and diarrhea bother me a little (like everybody else). I sure will appreciate any kind of a hot cooked meal from now on. Even the slop which we used to get on those tin mess trays would be food for a king.

I enjoyed a wonderful (and almost forgotten) sensation today. I brushed my teeth! It lifted my morale some in fact. I found a brand new German toothbrush, boiled it in a C-ration can, borrowed some toothpowder, and then brushed away. Man, it feels good now. Now next if I can find enough water, I might consider washing my face and shaving. Gosh, if I keep this up I'll be garrison.

No packages yet but I've got my fingers crossed. Please send me a box of eats. Don't forget a cheap pen for me too. So long for now.

Shinji

22 Nov. 1944, France

Dear H and E,

At last I got a real souvenir, one that I always wanted to get. It's a beautiful storm-trooper officer's cap with gold eagles and wreaths and braid on it still intact. I put it in a box and sent it home today and boy I sure hope you will get it. I got it in the building that used to be the storm troopers' headquarters. What a layout! Huge Nazi eagles in front of the building, swastika banners, and Hitler pictures in every room. They left in such a hurry that I guess they didn't have time to put their hats on, because mine is still clean. Also left behind beautiful officer's boots (which were too big to send home) and swastika arm bands. I also put in the box two officer's belts which are brand new. I found them in a closet. Please save this stuff for me will you. I know just where to put it in my shop.

I just remembered that I forgot to ask you for a package in this letter so please send me a package of eats.

Please tell the folks that I am O.K. and will write as soon as I can. That's all for today,

SHINJI

P.S. Please put my pipe and some pipe cleaners in your next eats package.

LETTERS BY TSUCHIDA

France, 25 Nov. 1944

Dear H and E,

Yipee! I got two of your packages today. One was a Christmas package and the other one was with the soap and toothpaste. The outsides of the packages were beat up but the contents were intact and O.K. Now what was the idea of the perfume and powder! I'm afraid you take anything I say too literally but thanks just the same. We gave it to some German girls for some apples.

The candy was swell. That small size box of Mrs. Stevens' candy was the ideal size to put in an overseas package. The nuts were a luxury too good to believe out here. The fruit juice was good and I hope you send more.

When we were just new overseas and still combat virgins you might say, I asked you for soap and stuff like that. Little did I know, so I guess I better tell you now that you don't have to send toilet articles any more. For the simple reason that you cannot carry things like that in combat and that you don't wash very often anyway. I don't have a single article on me (except probably my glasses and wrist watch) that I started out with. Everything else has been thrown away, lost, or abandoned as excess stuff to carry. When we do have a chance to wash we usually go around here and there and borrow razors, soap, etc. I have been using bandages for towels. It's against regulations of course but violated by all medics. In spite of all this I do miss my own personal toothbrush which I can carry in my pocket someplace I believe. So would you please send me a toothbrush with a holder. If you can find one of these one-piece celluloid holders that covers just the brush end, well and good.

Along with our regular supplies (ammo, food, and clothing) they have a sort of a supplementary ration which includes cigarettes, candy, razor blades, soap, matches. Normally these rations should get to us about once a week but since things aren't normal out here we do not see them sometimes. These rations are free to front line men and theoretically they should give each man one pack of cigarettes a day, one penny Hershey bar, one stick of gum, one box of matches, and one bar of soap per squad, one razor blade, one toothpaste tube, shaving soap per squad. So when we do get these rations I trade cigarettes for candy. But since we don't wash or shave or brush teeth very often, these supplies more than take care of our toilet needs. So that's why you don't have to send me any more soap.

Our division is off the secret list now so please keep an eye open in case any mention is made of us in the papers or radio. The only news we get out here is through the Stars and Stripes, an ETO Army paper. It is very interesting to read about our deeds in the papers.

Who says the medics aren't in there? Sometimes we are ahead of the line companies. Once we read in the papers that such and such a town was taken by our army. If they only knew the story as Warren and I know it. This certain town was still under fire, hot with snipers and burning buildings but we had to get some cover for our casualties so we dragged into town and into a building with our wounded. So the next morning when the troops came in we were there to greet them. And were we glad to see them! But procedures like this are not uncommon now when we have to go into town even before it is occupied by our troops.

I am feeling fine and my health is O.K. My cold is not bothering me and my stomach still yields to a good appetite so what more can a man ask. I had the last piece of shrapnel taken out of my hand tonight and the procaine is beginning to wear off now so I will sign off. So long for now,

SHINJI

P.S. Please send a box of eats, with jams, fruits, juices.

Dec. 3, 1944

Dear H and E,

We had a big mail call today ranging from Oct. 24 to Hime's letter of Nov. 19. I'm glad the mail is getting to us again. Comes in spurts. Thanks for writing so often. Just write about home and you'll keep me happy.

No! No! No! don't send me a heat pad. I can't use things like that. After waiting for precious packages, I would hate to see that room go to waste. As I wrote before, I don't have any of my original equipment left. Here is what I wear now to give you an idea. They might be considered the *absolute* absolute necessities: a pistol belt with canteen, aid kits, shovel, and raincoat. All this is hung on the pistol belt. We long ago shed our field packs (the thing that looks like a knapsack) and pup tent, poles, pegs, mess gear. I keep just a fork in my pocket. I even lost my raincoat (and I really hated to give that up) when we wrapped it around a casualty. Thanks anyway for your consideration but there is no substitute for dry weather and dry clothes. (To an infantryman just the opportunity to take off his shoes at night is considered a luxury, and but rare!)

Just one more complaint and then I'll quit. (I'm being choosy I know but I hope you'll be lenient.) Please don't you dare send any rice crackers! Anything that resembles ration crackers is sickening. Good ol' white bread is like cake out here. But crackers, crackers, crackers! It's maddening!

Instead of complaining so much maybe I ought to give you some hints. "Peanuts, popcorn and soda pop!" should explain it. Just make it a variety in each box of goodies instead of 5 lbs. of peanuts or 5 lbs. of any one thing.

So long for now,

SHINJI

P.S. Please send a box of eats.

[Such a request as this is very familiar—to the eleven million men in the armed forces who regularly made it and to the twenty-two million parents who regularly received it. Postal authorities required evidence of a serviceman's desire for a package, and the postscript was the most prominent place in which to express it. Will Tsuchida fulfilled this requirement in nearly every letter he wrote, not because he was underfed but because he, like every G.I., cherished the package from home—particularly when he had been subjected for too many days to the theoretically balanced diet of straight C-ration or, worse, straight K's. Most of the requests are omitted from the letters here; they may nevertheless be presumed.—D. R. B.]

5 Dec. 1944

Dear H and E,

Mail caught up with us again. Expect ours to be censored more strictly from now on as we have been told today.

Thank Mary for her swell letter. Let me know more about the Lt. she knows. She told me the trees in front of the apartment are pretty bare, and of the wooden board walks in the Midway, meaning that it's really winter in Chi. You better go ice-skating more often this winter.

No, I don't care if you tell me your troubles about things in the states because that's what I want to hear about—the states, and in order to do that you certainly couldn't leave out your troubles. And on top of that, it's humorous sometimes. I know you folks are rooting for me genuinely so please don't feel any reluctance in telling me about any extravagances (if there are any left) that you may indulge in. I enjoy reading of them because it's just that much more to look forward to when we get home.

Tell me more about your friend Mr. Rosedale from Berkeley. Gee he must be an important guy to have engineered Corregidor.

My gosh but I didn't know I wrote Belle anything out of the ordinary. Now that's the trouble with some of the people back home. One of my friends got a letter from the states asking if we had any heat in our barracks! But I do remember when I wrote to Belle it was right after I had pieced together a guy's leg in one of the pillboxes we were in about a month ago. A mortar shell had landed near his hole and it split the muscles of his leg wide open. There was a pool of blood around his leg and as I began to cut his trousers and shoes away, the fleshy meat just plopped out. It took four envelopes of sulfa powder to cover the wound, and then I just picked up the meat with my fingers and wrapped it up with several compress bandages. How they would work on his leg back in the evacuation hospitals is beyond me. He didn't even complain. In fact his only concern was that we didn't risk *our* necks to take him out of his hole. And then we had mail that night, which included a letter from Belle wondering "how do you like places like Paris?" Well I answered her letter but I wasn't feeling too happy that night.

When you asked me in your letter whether I wanted to be an M.D. after the war, I suppose you meant it very casually. You know my answer is—hell no! My branch of service now was no choice as you may remember how we were shoved around back in 1942.

Nope, haven't seen any correspondents in our neck of the woods yet. We had one in the aid station a couple of months ago but I think the BS artists took care of him.

Thanks for buying the records for Bessie. Did you give it to her for Christmas?

Smitty helped me discover something a couple of nights ago. "Let's Dance," BG's theme, is from "An Invitation to a Dance" by Carl Maria von Weber, a 19th century composer. He was playing the original when I recognized the theme and we were both quite surprised by it but close note-by-note examination reveals them to be identical. Go to the nearest record shop and mooch a free listen.

I got a package from Mrs. Schenker, and also one from her neighbor. I guess the quickest way to thank them is through Kiyoko so please tell her the next time you see her that they came. This neighbor of Mrs. Schenker is the "K-K-Katy" that compiles the "Knapsack Library" for servicemen. She sent three of them to me which was very nice of her.

I got a haircut a few days ago from a soldier in K company but what it amounts to is a G.I. clip all over. At long last.

Yes, we know quite well that the Germans are rats so you don't have to worry about any of my sympathy going to them. Far from it. We have seen enough—first hand. The only thing that holds us back is reprisal to our prisoners. But we still have plenty far to go to catch up with dirty Heinie work. Someday I will tell you about a boy in our detachment who lost his mother in a concentration camp. He has the real story.

Wham! Coming in again.——Back in my chair now.

Thanks for the clippings on the 44th Division. I asked my Lt. and he says we can tell you that we are near the Saar Basin.

So long for now, SHINJI

Dec. 6, 1944

Dear H and E,

Well, Eiichi, I see how hard you are trying to figure out where we are so I hope you got the letter in which I told you we are in the Seventh. No, we are not in Germany but we are farthest into Europe as you can see in your papers. And these mountains don't help matters any.

I guess we are about the most rummaging army there is. Any time we hit a town or a house we just tear it apart. They have warned us several times about looting and being punished by court-martial but still it goes on. But yesterday our rummaging through civilian property paid off. We found a picture of a kid in the German army in his uniform among the family pictures. We forgot about it until yesterday afternoon we noticed the family who lives here herding a guy around in civilian clothes. They brought him in, fed him, and then let him wash up. We were standing around the kitchen stove when he came in. The family was trying to act casual about it and we didn't notice this "just another civilian" until we remembered that picture and we all agreed on the similarity. So while one of the fellows went to notify the CIC [Counterintelligence Corps] the rest of us decided to do our best to make him stay in the kitchen. Well the people wised up I think because all of a sudden they got nervous and this kid grabbed his hat and headed for the door. We were wondering what to do when just at that time two MP's from the CIC came around the corner and nabbed him. We found out today that he was the guy in the picture and that he was in the German army but when they retreated he ditched out in civilian clothes. So geographically this may still be France, but that's all!

It may be near Christmas by the time you get this so my best to you. There are plenty of fir trees in these mountains but I would much rather see them in the front parlor. Sometimes we see small fir trees mounted on the tanks. Comedians you know. So, Merry Christmas to you and the neighbors—Helen, Mary, Mo, Mrs. Brandt—and I sure wish I could be there!

SHINJI

P.S. Did you get my French Christmas cards yet? I bought them in the town of Nancy.

Dec. 8, 1944

Dear H and E,

More of this German paper. Well three years ago today it was a Monday that I first went down to the recruiting center in S.F. But you didn't know it though. And I tried to study for my physics final that night too. That sure was a mess, wasn't it?

Well you can stop worrying, for a while anyway. The war in this neck of the woods has become mobile and we are going from one town to the next. We are sleeping in buildings, standing or otherwise, which beats the wet ground, and we are dried out, and they are getting hot meals to us (last two days anyway so we still can cross our fingers on that) and best of all nobody in our companies has been hurt this week. So what more can we ask right now, compared to those terrible days a few weeks ago.

[Censored]

This kind of war is not too bad when you have them on the run and keep them running. It's from town to town and as long as we can always get buildings for the men I'll be happy. Here's hoping we have no more counter-attacks.

Last night we had what I would call one of the most pleasant evenings we have had yet and that is saying a lot. It didn't require wine, women and vocal stretching but just some good people we met. It's all very confusing because some towns can be pro-Nazi to the last swastika and then the next can be anti. Well we came to this town yesterday and didn't get any outward greetings, which didn't make any difference to us. So we started to force a door in and only then did a lady come out. We sat in their front room and via sign language and dictionary asked them if we could build a fire. She got the idea fine because she brought in chairs and built the fire herself. We gave her our cans of ration which she put in a pot and cooked for us, and also some potatoes and onions which we peeled for some French fries. And then that great event of eating at a table out of plates. Next we learned about this town. At last, this is the kind of people we always wanted to meet. This woman is in her early thirties, has two boys, a husband in the French navy missing since Oran. She is fervently patriotic (good, because we were beginning to doubt these people) and very intelligent, well up on current events. Here's the story she told us about the townspeople. The Germans have been working on their positions here for at least five years and have used these grounds for their maneuver area. So they know the land like a book. The Germans forced her two boys to dig trenches along with other civilian men, women and children. So she had to hide them. Then they hung two farmers who didn't like the idea of working for the Heinies. One by one they began to leave for the hills to form partisan groups. And then two years ago a British and then an American paratrooper landed here to organize their guerrilla warfare. They shot up all kinds of vehicles with the inevitable sacrifice of leading citizens as hostages, beginning with the priest whom they accused of observing from the church steeple. But the partisans here have done their best work since D-Day this summer in observing for our P-47 fighter-bombers, which they call the "jabo." (The kids yell "jabo! jabo!" every time a P-47 flies over. It's supposed to be the German abbreviation for dive bomber.) Every time a vehicle no matter how small, or a train (even one box car) would appear in this town, sure as shinola a P-47 would pop up to strafe the hell out of it. Their observation was supposed to be so good that a few weeks ago a lone SS man was going down the street and sure enough a "jabo" appeared and strafed him.

We got all this from her, sitting around the fire munching apples which the kids brought up in baskets. We believe her because of her enthusiasm and sincerity. And we ate it up because it was really out of the books.

I got your letter today with those two pills in it. Thanks for your thought but our stomachs are really haywire and beyond indigestion.

No packages yet but we are "expectant."

The weather is cold and numbs the fingers so I hope you have sent the gloves.

So long for now,

SHINJI

P.S. Now she is showing us her pictures and even her love letters (we must look timid I guess). The first love letter she got from her husband was just a blank page with her name on it. This has been explained to us as the highest degree of European sentiment. Ahem. Now to reality, harsh as it is—please send me a box of eats.

Dec. 15, 1944

Dear H and E,

Hello folks. Hope you didn't mind the break in correspondence because we were roughing it again for a while. I am all right, feeling O.K. But I am feeling plenty tired now and as soon as I finish this letter I will roll up in a corner and go to sleep. Here's hoping nobody gets hurt for a while.

Now it's the damn pillboxes, to make it just that much harder. Not that what I say makes any difference but when will all this end? A bunch of good American kids have to go through hell for a mess of concrete and steel. It sure is no bargain. You may be interested in these pillboxes so here's what they are like.
[censored]
the only way to describe it. Camouflage is natural because the grass has grown right over the concrete.

Talk about your heroes, our demolition squad crawled up with TNT on their backs and blew the door in. And the infantry guys took a beating while they did it. Even the tanks had pulled back after their firing point-blank at the pillboxes had failed. But this one company of guys with just rifles had to stick it out. You figure it out. We can't.

After it quieted down a little we used the pillboxes to take care of the casualties. A few moments before we were cussing the thickness of the pillboxes, but when we were inside we were glad of it. It was a good place to work. I guess yesterday was about the noisiest day I ever spent. Artillery can really scream and I can see why a guy exposed to it long enough goes batty.

After we took care of our men we treated the Germans. They cry and moan more than our men, possibly for fear of being overlooked. Their cry of "kamerad! kamerad!" is known to us as a sign of surrender. Well, they were moaning "kamerad" so much I shot all of them full of morphine to quiet them down.

Got the California Monthly today and it sure was good to see it. Which reminds me, the other week I got my first issue of Life magazine but we were just moving out and I hadn't read it yet but was carrying it under my arm taking quick glances at it. Then on the road we got strafed by two 109's so when I dived in the ditch, the Life magazine fell right in a big puddle of mud.

No packages yet since those first two. I wonder what's holding them up. How many would you say you send a week? I hope you have sent me a pen of some kind by now because I am borrowing all the time.

I also need a new watch strap for the watch you gave me, Eiichi. Would you please look up the size in the catalog.

So long for now. Please write and send. How is my pipe tobacco pouch coming along?

SHINJI

Dec. 17, 1944

Dear H and E,

Big mail call today. Thanks. It's a cold day today but beautiful, so the air corps is out to give us a hand. We are still trying to crack the pillboxes and it's a beautiful sight to watch the P-47's dive bomb right over our heads. They seem to be oblivious to our fight on the ground down here; where we try to camouflage everything (involuntary in the case of mud) the air corps comes out in bright shiny planes painted with gaudy red paint on their tails and white invasion stripes on their wings, obvious as all hell. We all hope they do some good today.

You're right about Bill Mauldin's cartoons. They are really good and very very true. Incidentally his outfit the 45th Division [censored]. At one time one of their units relieved one of ours. Our men are getting to look like "Willie and Joe" too—bearded, dopey-eyed, hunchbacked, ragged, torn, and mud-caked. He plugs for the medics too.

So long for now,	SHINJI

20 Dec. 1944, 6 p.m.

Dear H and E,

I just got your letter with this stationery enclosed so I will be able to answer right here on the spot. It is a very good idea to enclose a stamp because they are very hard to get and it's a pleasure to write on this good paper.

Right now I am writing to you from "King" Company CP. ("King" is K in the phonetic alphabet.) It is just an old cellar with one end blown out and there is no building over us, just rubble. At one end of the room the Lt. is bending over his phone. It is getting dark so the riflemen are getting ready to go on their patrols, and that's when I'm glad I'm a medic because we don't have to go out on patrols. And it takes a lot of guts and fingercrossing for these squads. They load themselves down with hand grenades and automatic weapons only, because it's more sensible to throw a grenade than to shoot a rifle and give your position away. A patrol at night is almost synonymous with the phrase "I'm asking for it."

And it is plenty cold tonight but no fires allowed in here tonight because it would smoke us out and if we dropped the blankets covering the opening, our candle-lights would show. Contrary to the weather the situation is still hot because the German shells still land in here and you can hear their "burp" guns in the next draw. Just a few hours ago we had a barrage, with us as the target which means we are under observation and that this building is zeroed in by their guns. Here's one of those freak occurrences. One of the shells landed right in front of the doorway where there were three men standing. The man nearest the door was blown in but unhurt, and the same for the second man. But the third man who was behind the first two got a nasty shrapnel wound in his leg. We can't explain it but it's just one of those things that happens so fast nobody can figure it out. This cellar was hit several times (but nothing came through the top) all from the front so everybody is jittery about going out. Everybody in the room is covered with red dust and you can still smell the cordite in the air. It is a sharp pungent smell and whoever makes up that list of psychological associations with certain smells should include that of fresh burned powder. It is always a sure sign that a place is still hot.

Well everybody is wrapping up in whatever they have for the night and I will try to sleep too. I have some blankets which I took off the jeep-ambulance so I am lucky. As for evacuation we are very fortunate in this place because there is a road that comes right to this ex-building, so the jeep can drive right to here from the aid station. But the Germans know there is a road here too so they shell it every time they think there is something going over it. Our driver was the first one to use this road (as usually is the case for the medics) and he took a big chance or gamble on the possibility of mines. But it isn't the first time we have had to do this. Hell, the engineers are always a day late with their detectors. I think our driver is going to requisition a mine detector of his own, which isn't a bad idea.

Everybody has a bad cough and I know they have colds. This ground is hard and cold but you don't hear anybody in the infantry complaining because anything is better than a hole filled with mud and water. Gee but they groan a lot in their sleep. I wonder if I do, but according to Warren I don't. A rifleman just came over to me for some more diarrhea pills and I gave him some sulfaguanidine and bismuth tablets. He's going outside again now because I just heard the guard challenge him. Gee whiz, but everybody's got the runs. Including me.

Well goodnight for now. Hope it's a quiet night.

SHINJI

Dec. 25, 1944, 1200

Dear H and E,

Merry Christmas everybody, and I think it has been one so far. Because we are indoors and we have a stove and we had a hot breakfast this morning and because we even had services this morning. And that is plenty good considering the guys freezing in their foxholes right now just beyond the edge of town. I wish I knew the name of this town so I can say a year from now that I was at such and such a place. I will find out tonight as we leave, which I am sure we will, because every time I get just about comfortable we move out.

I'm wondering what kind of a dinner we will get today. For breakfast we had pancakes, sausage, cream of wheat, and marmalade. It was darn good despite the fact the marmalade froze on the pancakes, but I will eat pancakes with frozen marmalade and icicles in my coffee for the duration if they would promise me a cooked breakfast every morning. Boy what a difference on my stomach, which feels much better now.

Warren says thanks for writing to Jean which I guess you did when you sent the pictures. Incidentally, Warren was sent back for about a week because of a bad stomach and he came back yesterday with new clothes. We razzed his clothes more than envied them, but it won't take long to get them dirty out here.

Good news! One fruitcake from Mama and a box from Ruth day before yesterday. Sorry about the little tree but we were right in the midst of a big move and all I could do was to unwrap it. Gee but that was a shame so I hope you will prevent that sort of thing in the future. Please check Pop's address too. He had 1st Infantry instead of 71st. So long for now,

SHINJI

Christmas, 1944

Dear Folks,

We had services in a schoolhouse today full of shell holes. On a sign saying "Kindergarten" Smitty hung another one saying "Christmas Service, Protestant, at 1100." Inside, Smitty and the Chaplain had a fir tree decorated and we sat around it in little kiddie chairs. The carols and the organ sounded good.

SHINJI

28 Dec. 1944

Dear H and E,

Here's where I give the censor a bad time because my typing and captured typewriter is some combination.

Here is the Christmas that I had, which was not too bad considering the guys who couldn't leave their foxholes. We had a Christmas dinner that was plenty good—turkey, cranberry, potatoes, peas, and mince pie. And we had a building with a good stove. Out here you couldn't ask for more than that.

The holiday is over and we're back to K rations again. Damn it but do I hate the lousy K's! I can't even eat the candy in them. Some one suggested that they should put an Honorable Discharge in every millionth box of K's as an inducement to make the men eat them.

Warren got a Pfc. today, but something else also came out today that kind of put a dimmer on Warren's underrated rating. It's kind of a long story but I'll tell you part of it. Once upon a time there was a town by the name of Leintry, which at the time we knew it was quite hot, both physically and strategically. In fact it was so hot that the buildings were still burning and the snipers were not all cleared. We had plenty of casualties that night because it was right after an attack. Warren, Schubel, and I decided to use the buildings in this town for the wounded because we didn't know where our aid station was. We entered this town with our wounded from the side that our troops did not use, which also means that the road was not cleared and any damn thing could happen. We literally tiptoed into town and when the burning buildings cast their light on us we thought we could feel a hundred pairs of eyes on us. Altogether we had six casualties in a small room of a building which we later found out was the city hall. We took care of these guys with what we had in the dark, scoured up some hay and covered up everybody to keep them warm. We even used parts of our clothing, even our socks. We heard a million sounds and every one of them scared us. German 88 shells were bouncing down the street and we could see them hitting the building across the street. Then we heard someone outside who was apparently trying to figure out who *we* were. He spoke finally in English asking for the medics. It turned out that there were two more casualties at the other end of town so after getting these two we had eight guys to take care of altogether. One was a Lt. with a very bad sucking chest wound who showed great courage by limping and dragging himself into town. He moaned an awful lot and I can't seem to forget that even today. We found the Regimental OP operated by only two men who had a radio. Through them we contacted our aid station for some help. We waited and waited that night, really sweating it out for these eight guys. The incoming mail (German shells) and the burning building, which must have provided a perfect target, didn't help matters. We called up again two more times hoping that we could get better medical aid for the men. We had quite a mad time of it running around in the dark from one man to the other tending to them. At last about midnight we heard the motor of the ambulance crawling up the road on the "safe" side of town. We hoped that the driver wouldn't race his motor too loud because the Germans had been firing at vehicles on that road. Just about when the ambulance was going to go past the building we were in I ran out and hailed them. We got the casualties loaded and it was quite a load. A medical officer and a S/Sgt. technician from the aid station came up with this ambulance and they looked everybody over before we put them in the ambulance. After everybody was gone we went down into the cellar and went to sleep. The next day when the rest of the troops and the aid station came into town, we were there to greet them. The fellows told us that they thought we were lost until we radioed them, and they said we did a good job and asked us how we felt to be the first ones to occupy a town, and that sort of bull. And that's the story of the town of Leintry. Today we found out that the S/Sgt. technician and the medical officer who came up in the ambulance received the Bronze Star award for what they did in Leintry.

Someone once said, "Virtue is its own reward" but one Pvt. on going overseas has learned a different twist to that. Having personally seen so many acts of heroism by the men of the infantry overlooked for a just reward time and time again, I think it is quite obvious that virtue is overlooked and even eclipsed by the louder voice. In other words, nobody wants a medal, or even recognition for a deed, but it is a sad plight when an award depends on who writes it up.

Please buy a small box of air mail stationery (with stamps to accompany them) for Warren's birthday on Feb. 11th. I think I told you once before that our birthdays were a day apart. Also buy him a deluxe washrag (small) because he is nuts about them.

So long for now, hope you have a happy New Year. Will sing Auld Lang Syne to the Heinies to see what kind of a response we will get, which I can readily guess.

SHINJI

30 Dec. 1944

Dear H and E,

Hello folks again. It's not a genuine break but I am taking it easy today and am hoping that it will last for a little while. But you know the army so I am not banking on anything. I found a pot in a kitchen of a shelled-out building and cleaned it out so I can wash. There's an artesian well down the street with ice all over it where the water overflows but the spout is still giving out with water so now with a hot fire I'll have hot water in a few minutes. What I would really like to get is a haircut. It's way down over my ears and a pretty knotty affair. I had my last one in Normandy. I'll refer you to one of Mauldin's cartoons for a general idea of what my hair looks like.

Yesterday I got two packages, one from Kiyoko and another one from the Moody Church in Chicago. I guessed that maybe mama put in my name. Good for that. Gee, you know what, we had a bad rumor today and I was wondering. Some warehouse in New York where they have been keeping Christmas overseas packages was supposed to have burned down. Hope that none of ours were in there. Or did you hear any such rumors in the states?

Must remark on the feminine impressions we are getting as we go along. It is generally agreed that the women are getting better (said adjective "better" covering all points of feminine pulchritude), as we go in farther. You have probably heard a lot about the sturdy frauleins and to be quite frank with you I think they are raised for service. (What kind of service? Just look at the size of the farms.) The one we had at the last town where we had the beer parlor was quite a package. It may be that we have been away from civil life too long but I do think there is something to this "natural beauty" in the Ingrid Bergman-ish manner.

Thanks for the review on Carey McWilliams' book. Smitty showed me a copy of the review in PM which he gets regularly. Are you planning on getting it? It should be good but do you suppose the right people will read it.

Please keep writing and so long for now,

SHINJI

Jan. 2, 1945, 4:15 A.M.

Dear H and E,

Happy New Year folks, at this late date. I'm sorry I couldn't extend my greetings to you yesterday, which would have been more proper, but this is really the first chance I have had to try to write any letter in this new year.

You may remember in my last letter to you that I said I was enjoying a brief rest but didn't expect it to last very long. It didn't.

Writing to you now from the back room in the aid station. It's warm in here so I can appreciate the aid station for a change whereas I have always been criticizing it. In fact I was kind of proud of the medics in our battalion the past few days because we were up farther than the aid stations of the other two battalions in the regiment. Consequently we were taking care of everybody else's casualties.

Everybody is sleeping on the floor and in the chairs now. I suppose we'll be moving out by daybreak. Boy but everybody is tired, by the way they sleep. I guess I could stand and still go to sleep. This sort of thing has been going on for the past few nights. Why do they have to fight at night?

Well the New Year came in with a bang. The Germans even timed it to the minute. I wonder if they thought we would all be drunk on New Year's Eve or be off guard. They must have really planned for this party because they came dressed in white which blended well with the snow. The lousy Heinies—they will be so deliberate in some things. As if there were any rules in this war. I don't know how the papers back home treat these counter-attacks by the Germans but I guess you know that they are good, very good, at this game, and that we take a good shellacking sometimes. Thank God for our superiority in men and supplies. I'm glad we're on the winning side because it is rough enough on the offensive but imagine how hectic things would get if we were withdrawing every day.

My stomach is responding to K-rations like oil does to water. Had some rabbits cooked by the civilians here on New Years Eve which was very good. They are shelling us again now. It's a terrible sound. Everybody must be tired because nobody woke up.

Was on German soil three nights ago. Schubel and I went along as medics on a raid on a German OP about a thousand yards away from our lines. We were deep in the woods when we crossed the line and found a concrete marker. We checked the marker by reading it under a blanket and flashlight. Let me be crude for a moment and tell you what we did. The occasion called for a ceremony so both of us, in a typical army state of mind, urinated on German soil. The raid turned out to be a quiet one with a few shots fired, nobody hurt, and six prisoners. The prisoners claimed that they were part of the "stomach ulcer" battalion which we read about in the Stars and Stripes. I guess we aren't the only ones who have trouble with our stomachs. We made them carry our heavier equipment and litters back to our lines.

I got the catalog from the aeronautical university a few days ago but haven't looked at it too well yet. Thanks for sending it but I think I would prefer to go to a bigger school with some name to it. One of these days I'll make up my mind about what school I want to go to.

Getting sleepier so good night. Or is it good morning?

SHINJI

4 Jan. 1945

Dear H and E,

Hello again and another town, in the wrong direction. Mail has reached us at last so I have lots to answer. Your maps of France and Germany came also. I remember asking for them back in Normandy when I was eager about the army in general. To be honest with you, combat has taken most of that eagerness out of me.——— Nuts! Every time I start a letter they start shelling. I just came off the floor again. Boy am I jittery. Instead of getting better at the game we get worse as far as our nerves are concerned. Here we go again.———Back in my chair again. Gee but won't they ever quit. I know that every man in the regiment could feel twice as good if we could get a genuine rest in a rear area for about a week. With hot food. We can be in reserve at the front but that doesn't mean a rest usually because, as we have found out, we get committed more often and run into more trouble when we are in reserve than when we are on line. Enough of this.

They are still having sessions but not at the Dawn Club but some other place with which I am not familiar. But let me tell you of the session. Bill Bardin, our trombone man, was sitting in and there was a clarinetist from Oregon visiting so he sat in too. Well he was pretty good and fitted in the outfit pretty well, except he didn't know the classic tunes. So during one of the intermissions Bill took him into another room, with two bottles of beer, and began teaching him "Down by the River." Well they were blowing away with great enthusiasm and with such inspiration that pretty soon one by one they drew everybody into their room and before they knew it the session continued in that room. Ah, but to be back!

Still coming in. The whine of a shell is really bloodcurdling. But it doesn't end with just the sound of it.

SHINJI

8 Jan. 1945

Dear H and E,

Thanks again for the mail. Feel pretty well up to date on what goes on at home. And I got the news about California and us a few days ago via the Stars and Stripes. It was great news, but it still doesn't seem clean cut. So much damage seems to have been done already and in some cases unrepairable. You know how I feel about going home—a real home. If I knew that we could fix up a place for ma and pop, a real place with lawns and gardens and stuff like that, and a real definite place we could call home when I get out of the army, I believe I could fight twice as hard out here. Personally I don't see how these kids in the outfits like the 100th and 442d can fight as hard as they do with their parents still in the Relocation Camps. It all comes under the morale department; there's nothing that can give you a lift like the thought of going home again—if you have one. So Eiichi, in answer to your question whether I will be disappointed if it's not Berkeley my answer is no. I don't care where it is as long as it's in the U.S.A., although there is no other place like Berkeley. Anyway, don't let me press you on this because I think you have done a swell job already in getting the folks placed so well in Chicago. I have to thank you for that when I think of how bad it could have been. I want to go to school too so I will try to have some definite answer for you soon.

Mama and pop will be happy to know that their package with the candy and soap arrived yesterday so please phone them if this gets to you before theirs.

We are being shuffled around so much since yesterday that I don't know which way is the front. I don't even know what side the sun rises from—or care. But the great event yesterday was the showers, change of clothes, and movies. Yeah but I'm a new man today. My hair was so dirty and caked that it took a full minute of scrubbing before the lather came out. The grunts and groans of pleasure from bathing emitted by the men were strange and almost forgotten sounds. It was snowing like the devil outside of that little tent and there was a long line of dirty men waiting their turn. Every time the flap opened a lot of steam would come out and as one man came out another went in. That's the way we went to the show too, "Lady in the Dark." It was so damn good to hear the intro that it tickled me pink.

Then we get all wrapped up in the picture and when it's over, out of the barn we go back to the war. Ah, 'tis cruel. I wished as hard as I could for the after-show hamburger and shake but all I got was a draft of snow down my neck.

Live from day to day is what I say and I can't complain today. You can tell the difference on everybody, the way they talk a lot, horse around, and run around without their helmets. A man needs mental relief as much as physical.

Another rumor which belongs in the good news dept. if it's true is that the 71st Regt. is going to get a Presidential Unit Citation. And our medics got a commendation from Corps. Hope the Regt. gets the citation because it sure deserves it.

Don't forget the candles in the package. Just got your Christmas card, Helen and Mary's too. So long for now,

SHINJI

10 Jan. 1945

Dear H and E,

Got two packages today from you which should make you as happy as I am because I know you were sweating them out. I can't make out the dates on them so here are the contents which might identify them for you. One was a box of Mrs. Snyder's candy and the other was a damn good package, the best I ever got from home yet. It had several bars of candy, can of nuts, stationery, camphor ice, handkerchiefs, and a little of Eiichi's touch, lipstick! I forgot to mention the candles too, which came just in time. We ran out of captured candles about a week ago. Thanks for everything. Hoping that there is more to follow.

It's all very confusing. I'm writing in the kitchen of a middle-aged couple with the lamp in the middle of the table and they are sitting on the other side of the table. Warren is talking with them in his very best Wisconsin German. They have four small boys who we went sledding with this afternoon, who are in bed now. Their house is not big and they are what you call middle class. The mother must work long hours because she looks tired, had hands that are worn, a wet and soiled apron. The father has a wrinkled and weather-beaten face, and talks like a tired man except when he discusses the "boche" and then he uses wild gesticulations. This afternoon we knocked on their door and asked if we could use one of their rooms to sleep in. It was more hospitality than obedience to a uniformed soldier (to which they must have been accustomed when the Germans were here) that they invited us in and sat us down by the kitchen stove. They gave us their bedroom after we explained to them that all we wanted was floor space. But they insisted so tonight I guess we will sleep on a bed. She made coffee for us and hot milk, and promised to make cheesecake for us tomorrow. But here's what they are talking about to Burger. They know they are Germans in speech, mannerisms, heritage. But it's been small people like them that have had it hard since 1935. They have three older boys snatched into the German army. And as usual they haven't heard from them or about them. One of the boys was shot in the arm by the Germans before they took him away. He wrote his mother later that he lost the use of his fingers as a result but he is still in the army. Now she says when she looks at us we remind her of her boys. It must be pretty rough on her because she is crying, not slobbing all over us, but tears just well up in her eyes as she talks. We tell them that we are reading letters from home and she says the worst part is not knowing whether the boys are getting the letters they wrote to them. I unwrapped my packages on the table and of course they expressed amazement at the contents and the fact that they could be sent to us. (The kids went for the candy, but they didn't get all of it.)

Now here's what is so confusing (bad choice of word, maybe thought-provoking is better). When we are on the lines we cuss and hate with all our might the Heinie. I was just wondering how many cases there were of families broken up like this one here. (Hitler will never know the misery he's caused.) But here we sit in this kitchen with these people, and probably fighting their sons. Never can figure out how the Germans can force their Polish, Slavish, and Russian troops to fight for them. Must have a knife threatened over their relatives and loved ones. But then from our point of view, why don't they shoot over our heads? Yeah, as we always say, if it's in a Heinie uniform shoot the hell out of it. The whole thing is a mess so why stop to think about the circumstances. They kill us so we do the same.

The father is telling us of the time when they had Russian prisoners here. The Germans made them dig ditches and the Russians were beaten with clubs until they fell. They were so hungry they ate worms off the ground, he says. Civilians who sympathized left food in certain spots until they were caught and punished likewise. Once the town was bombed by American planes and the Russians went through the houses unguarded, looking for food madly, even eating raw horse flesh. I guess the war has certainly been here.

Thanks again for packages.

SHINJI

13 Jan. 1945, Sunday

Dear H and E,

Still "enjoying" myself to the best of circumstances but my fingers are always crossed. The men are feeling better now than they have in a long time. Wow, but is it cold!

The lady here washed all our clothes and has been making things darn comfortable around here. First time that I have had ironed clothes on in a long time.

Sunday is a big day in the life of these people. They start Saturday night scrubbing the kids, brushing off Sunday clothes. Mama is baking bread for the next week and papa is cleaning a rabbit for today's dinner. Then they get all dressed for church. The kids in this town are really cute, cold air must make their cheeks so rosy. And that goes for the older girls too who are a bit of the "ja, gute!"

Boy, I sure am going to hate to leave this place. It's hard to think of their boys in the German army but I guess that will have to come in the c'est la guerre dept. The people have made this break so pleasant that it is sort of a stimulus or revival to the thought that the little people didn't go for the new order too well.

The kids here get a kick out of us I guess because they show us off to their neighbors. The little girl wakes up several times at night to make sure that we haven't left yet; so we call her name, "Christina," to let her know we are still here.

Rumors of a shower and movie so I will start looking up some soap now. Will let you know what the movie is later. So long for now,

SHINJI

P.S. Please send a package of eats!

22 Jan. 1945

Dear H and E,

Sure was glad to hear from you in today's mail, because the mail recently hasn't been reaching us. Two more packages came, one from you and one from Riyo. Please thank Riyo for me. Your package had the Life magazine edition called a "Letter to G.I.'s," which was very good, and Riyo's package also had some magazines, so now we have something to read.

Please do not forget the candles in the packages. Also pipe cleaners. In one of the towns we went through recently there was a candle factory (which is still capable of making candles, strangely) so I bought ten, the limit, for 20 francs. They must be undergoing a boom because all the G.I.'s are buying candles. At present you would see most of the guys with candles sticking out of all their pockets, packs, gas mask carriers, etc.

I wish I could answer all your questions about that New Year's day fracas but they would only censor it so I guess it will have to keep. But I think it's all right to say that we were so damn close and thick that it was possible to talk with them. One of my medic friends who speaks German was telling them to surrender and bring their wounded over. I guess you know how they answered us. We still think they were doped up. Enclosed is an SS collar patch which is symbolic in more than one way. The mention of SS troops used to scare us once but now we call them the Sad Sacks, or the Selective Service boys, or the Super S—ts. I have been told that the SS, or the Elite Guard, are all volunteers and they were the ones who were responsible for most of the atrocities in the occupied countries and other varied jobs which called for dirty work. I always wondered and doubted about the story that when they volunteered they signed their names with blood but one prisoner admitted that it was true. Nasty boys, aren't they? Incidentally, that boy I mentioned a few letters back who lost his mother in a German concentration camp went to pieces when he saw our first SS soldier. He went up to the prisoner and slapped him across his face with the back of his hand (a European touch I believe) and began screaming into his face in German which I couldn't understand. I believe he wanted to shoot him even though he is a medic. When we cooled him down later we told him we would not object to his killing any Germans out on the fields—but not near the aid station. Even now he feels that it is his fault that his mother's death has not been avenged.

Thanks a lot, Hime, for the articles by *the* Robt. Hutchins. All my friends who plan to go back to school have read it and are giving much thought to it. Will read the Round Table tonight. So long for now,

SHINJI

France, 24 Jan. 1945

Dear H and E,

The weather is still plenty cold and the snow of course is inevitable. The whole landscape can change overnight. Then a shell pushes that around some more. Must be confusing for these company runners who have to remember trails.

We went through a "big" town some time ago which was big enough to warrant a street named after Adolf Hitler. So one day I was walking down a street which had all the appearances of the main drag and on one corner I looked up at the street sign. There it was, big as daylight—"Adolf Hitler Strasse." It was too good to resist and I could just envision it hanging on the wall in my shop. So I rolled a barrel up to the sign and went to work on the screws. Pretty soon I had a civilian audience (it was a main thoroughfare after all) and their comments were mixed. Two old geezers started saying "nicht, nicht!" meaning leave it alone but the rest of the people shut them up and began encouraging me and I think they wanted me to take all the signs down. Well I stepped down from the barrel with the sign under my arm and I'll be darned if they didn't come up to me and want to shake my hand and that sort of thing. I wish I could have stayed there longer. That's all for now,

SHINJI

France, 28 Jan. 1945

Dear H and E,

Today is Sunday and I know it is because Smitty says so—and he should know. Come to think of it, I haven't attended a service since Christmas and that can be blamed on everybody including me.

Nothing exciting today except two prisoners and the way they surrendered. They came with their hands clasped over their heads yelling "kamerad!" It seems nobody noticed them so they went from door to door looking for somebody to "capture" them. In an interview later they said they left their holes after their officer went to sleep. One fellow was about 39, with a family and one hand crippled, which goes to show that most of them have the basic fear of the Gestapo harming their families. So long for now,

SHINJI

France, 30 Jan. 1945

Dear H and E,

The snow is still piling up here and without a doubt the most I have ever seen. But here is some consolation—it is not the coldest place I have been in, thinking specifically of Minnesota. The fact still remains, however, that the circumstances under which an infantryman must fight just automatically lead to his concluding that there is no spot on earth which could be called ideal.

Here's something people back home never see—the fantastic sight of hundreds and hundreds of bombers flying hour on hour, at such a high altitude that you can't see them or hear them. All you can see is the vapor trails. The vapor trails of, say one flight, converge into one big vapor trail which has the appearance of a white cloud pointed at one end. So the illusion you get is the weird sight of hundreds of small white "clouds" all pointing in one direction. Then there are thin, fine streaks of white which dart in and out of the bigger vapor trail clouds. These apparently must be the fighter escorts' vapor trails.

Back down to earth to "our" war. Every so often a single P-47, or a pair, will circle around us and then strafe or bomb our lines. These are German pilots in captured planes, and it's always an uncomfortable feeling to have a doubt about the identity of the *pilot* when we are certain about the identity of the plane. The same goes for a lot of other American equipment which has been captured, such as jeeps, halftracks, liaison planes, etc.

Eiichi, from here on concerns men's underclothing so if you think it may bring a touch of crimson to Hime's cheek you better tell her to stop here. Your comment on certain physiological processes that take place when one is scared enough is quite true. I should know because it has happened to me. Once when my stomach was quite jumpy (after weeks of eating canned rations) it didn't take too much encouraging to make them move. Well one day we were pinned down by 88's which were screaming down closer and closer—and that did it. When I got up the seat of my pants was quite, shall we say, moist. I wasn't wearing my "long johns" then but my summer shorts, so I got my scissors out and cut them off of me. It seems funny now when I think of it but I didn't laugh then. So long,

SHINJI

France, 9 Feb. 1945

Dear H and E,

I sent two packages home today. One of them was that street sign. Cross your fingers because it's so big and I may have trouble having it accepted. I wrapped it in a German blanket because it seemed to be the best thing to absorb the shocks. The other package is a small one with a German EM belt and a pair of SS officer's gloves. Incidentally, on the buckle of the Heinie belt is the inscription "God be with us" which is out of place with them, don't you think? Which proves their inconsistency and shows that the previously considered stoneheartedness of the Nazi army yielded to the whims (?) of their soldiers in this pseudo-religious touch. I might mention another thing here about the Krauts. We are often told how impassionate the Heinies are, yet I would say that every one of them carries a small mirror, fingernail file, nail clips, comb (sometimes even a hairbrush), tweezers, and similar items in their pockets. Some of them are real dandies with long, well-kept hair, and it's not strange to see freshly caught prisoners combing their hair unconcernedly in the prison camps. Getting off the track here. The story behind the gloves. They are fur lined and too clumsy to use for me so I asked if anybody else needed them and it seems that nobody does so I will send them home as souvenirs. On New Year's day I patched up the buttocks and arms of an SS officer (a Lt.) and in order to work on the arms I took his gloves off. I couldn't get them on again (as if I would trouble myself to) so he said something to the effect that I could keep them. It burned him up no end to be captured, by the way he acted, but he still seemed to have some gratitude for the medical attention.

Snow has thawed some and it rains about every six hours to make the place a sea of mud again. I would prefer snow to this if I knew it wouldn't have to melt.

Am feeling fine and in good health. SHINJI

12 Feb. 1945

Dear H and E,

Well, here it is again. Today makes my fourth birthday in the army. Let's see, the first one was in Camp Grant, second in Minnesota, third at ASTP in Missouri, and now the fourth in France. But what a birthday this one is—not even a letter from home but I have my fingers crossed yet because it's only 7 P.M. now. Even though some guys have been in the army even five, ten or more years, I definitely have had enough and that great day won't be soon enough.

Sometimes the thought of my best years slipping by, and the fact that I would be graduating from Cal this June if it weren't for this war, is almost unbearable. I get an itch to hit the books sometimes and then at other times I wonder whether I should get wrapped up in a job, get married, and go through that routine. At present the go-finish-school side is most dominant. But I am quite sure that I will take some advantage of the veterans' bill of rights.

Ah here comes the mail! Time out. Yours were from Jan. 24, 25, 28, Feb. 2 and 4. And the best news of all is your job offer in Berkeley. If you leave in March, I will be expecting a Berkeley postmark some time in April. Boy that sure will be swell. You are right about Pop and Mom—stay put! For the present anyway. And I hope, Hime, that you will finish at the U. of Chicago.

I am going to cut this short tonight and take it down

to the aid station right away. We had PX rations this morning, four cigars, two candy bars, one-half can fruit juice per man. No beer. I'm trading cigars for candy. Also saw a sultry thing called "To Have or To Have Not" this morning. Don't worry about me.

SHINJI

LETTERS BY TSUCHIDA

Feb. 19, 1945

Dear H and E,

Here I am again after a little lapse in the letter writing. So much has happened and is happening that I don't know where to begin in telling you. I have been cramming your letters in my pockets as fast as I got and read them. The events were exciting as naturally such circumstances are but it was nothing to crave for. That cold feeling was in my stomach all the time and I'm just getting over the jitters now. I will readily admit that I get scared and so will everyone else here. But right now I'm all washed up and just had a cup of coffee so I feel the best I have in the past few days. After I finish this letter I will hit the sack and sleep a couple of hours until noon. Boy I'm so tired I could go to sleep standing up. We were running around most of the night.

Well Burger and I were first medics into town again, if that means anything (and apparently not much to the people in the aid station and I will tell you why). This time we went in right behind the tanks and it wasn't quite the place for a medic to be now that we come to think of it. There's no rule in the books that says we have to stay that close behind but we were going through an orchard full of mines and the idea was to go through the tank tracks where if it was safe enough for a tank it was safe enough for us to walk. We were crouched abreast with the infantrymen who held their guns in readiness at port and in front of us was the tanks, and the Heinies in front of them. If any of our men got hit then, we could have had a litter under him before he hit the dirt. The din was terrific and if I could have a penny for every shell that was fired I would be a rich man.

Well the smoke kept pouring in from our flank where our artillery was dropping smoke shells. One of those shells landed short and we got sprayed with mud clods full of white phosphorus. That was, for a change, just like the movies. The Heinies were flushed from one building to the next. We worked on a guy in a crater hole and then took him to the nearest house that was cleared. This will probably be censored but we sure could have used some plasma then. We stopped a tank and asked the tankers if they were carrying any, which they do sometimes, but they didn't. The tankers radioed back to our CP to notify our aid station to send some plasma up. We held our building while the rest of the troops went down the street from cellar to cellar. By this time some of the smoke had lifted at our end of town and we watched the prisoners being taken back. A bunch of kids for the most part. Here's an example of how much concern they have for us sometimes. Our aid-station jeep finally showed up (no plasma) and our medical sergeant bawled us out for not having taken care of some casualties in some other companies to which we weren't even attached. Boy that sure burns us up. They don't even know what companies we are with sometimes. We don't want any praise for doing our work but when we don't have any existence to the people in the aid station, morale goes ker-plunk!

Thanks for all your letters. Am awaiting news about your new job. May the Russians end this quick and the same for the Pacific front.

So long for now. Am feeling fine and O.K. and very sleepy.

SHINJI

21 Feb. 1945

Dear H and E,

Waiting around for something to happen so it is a good chance to write home. Pulled some stuff out of my pockets today and found letters of Jan. 29 and Feb. 7 from you. But here is something I should tell you first. It came! Last night I went back to the aid station to find your Jan. 9th package. Yanked all the wrappings off and found that beautiful bottle of coke lying in there. It was a sight très belle. I take back everything I ever said about the impractical shape of the coke bottle back in the states. It's the most graceful thing that I have seen for a long time. I have not opened it yet. Not all the boys are in yet and I want them to get a look at it before draining the contents. A slight hunch tells me that I will become very popular upon opening the bottle, but sudden like. Thanks for sending it, it did the trick quite well. I am good for another two weeks or so. What I mean is sometimes our morale hits rock bottom and you become quite tired of it all. And then suddenly something you read, or hear—like Smitty's piano,—or a crazy thing like a bottle of coke from home will snap you out of it.

I think it is all right to tell you about how two of our boys won a 14-day pass to Paris, two bottles of whiskey, and the Silver Star award (in their order of relative importance). Well these two boys volunteered to knock out two German tanks which were banging away at our lines. After dark they crept up to the tanks, jammed a carbine rifle down the tank's machine gun barrel to make it incapable of firing. The tanks were pretty well buttoned up so they couldn't use hand grenades. They stepped back and fired their bazookas. Fortunately their first shots were good, otherwise their bazooka flash would have given them away. They sure deserve whatever they can get and that still couldn't be what they should get. Yep, nothing is too good for these guys.

The weather is unpredictable and there is nothing more futile than cursing the rain. Am feeling O.K. and hope I can avoid my usual spring cold.

SHINJI

22 Feb. 1945

Dear H and E,

The packages are coming in fine—one the day before yesterday and two yesterday. All of them had a bottle of coke in them which made them extraordinarily good packages. I passed the coke bottles as far as they would go which meant just about a swallow for everybody, but everyone who did get a taste did so in a state of rapture. Of course the hardier ones among us wished it was stronger stuff like Scotch or something but let me assure you on behalf of this platoon that just the sight of a coke bottle made all concerned a few degrees happier.

The sun is out today for which I wouldn't trade a million dollars. But everything from ankle down is still mud and the artillery wooshing by spoils any feeling of serenity. And these orphaned cows I told you about wander out to the lines sometimes but I'm afraid the only thing they will find are some mines or trip wires.

I am gradually becoming aware of the fancy lettering on your letters to me. Is that a special rubber stamp? It photographs well on V-mail, giving a de luxe touch to an otherwise G.I. product. Anyway, it attracts a lot of attention and everyone who handles the mail has some "Gee, lookit!" remark. Which brings up another point. My obscure first name has become quite prominent now and there are the usual questions on how to pronounce it. Most of the riflemen address medics as "Doc" and I am no exception. But ever since

I acquired "Will" it has been that to my friends in the army. Especially out here where frequent personnel change-overs are one of the products of front line warfare, quick and simple name recognition helps a lot.

That's about all for now. Am feeling fine, healthy and dirty. So long,

SHINJI

P.S. Please send a package of eats!—and candles.

Mar. 5, 1945

Dear Hime,

In writing that date just now up in that corner I realized how long it has been since I wrote last. About a week, by my memory and without the aid of a calendar, which I should have etched on the walls of my foxhole in my best Bastille-imprisoned scratchings. The life and discomforts of a hole in the ground—wow, it is miserable! (I used "wow" trying to inject a spirit of vim, vigor, and vitamins into this letter but in reality they don't exist in my physical body any more.) I hope I didn't worry you to any great extent because I am all right and can still look forward to this thing actually ending.

Eiichi should well be on his way by now. I hope everything works smoothly for him. I wish I could have shared some of the responsibility of all the moving the family has undergone since the war began. I can't thank you enough, Hime, for shouldering most of this burden for Eiichi and me. But I'm afraid I will still have to admit I'm in the dark yet on most of the undertakings.

From the exciting moments dept.: While sticking our heads out of our holes the other morning before dawn we saw our friends from across the line approaching us. We held our fire until they hit our barbed wire defense in front of our holes. Then in best movie fashion our machine guns clipped most of their legs off. The two who weren't hurt didn't know which way to run so I began yelling at the top of my voice in my best "Stars and Stripes" German, "Kommen sie hier!" Shocked by either the machine guns or my German, they stopped, and I ran out to them and knocked their helmets off to indicate surrender. They were all SS Germans but quite willing to surrender. I patched up the wounded and they were tickled pink. Acting like a hardened veteran I refused their handshakes. Tough ain't I?

We have a place a few hundred yards behind the lines where we take turns and go to, to wash up and dry our feet. I am writing from there now. The infantryman is probably the most appreciative person in the world to any comforts offered. One man here is expressing delight in soaking his feet in warm water— "I guess I'll wash my feet one at a time to make it last longer."

So long, SHINJI

Mar. 9, 1945, France

Dear Hime,

Back to the warmth of the aid station where I am thawing myself out from head to toe. Here is the reason for the war's not being for old men, if it must be for anyone. Last night in the driving rain we had several hills to climb. The slopes of these hills were deeply rutted by tank tracks full of rain water to knee depths. The mud sucked us down and the men, loaded down with tremendous loads, fell frequently. It was a miserable march and required all the stamina of a normal living person, let alone a front line meager-fed soldier. Breathing was hard and men panted painfully. The aid man usually brings up the rear, so pretty soon I noticed a small commotion where one man fell, and then I came upon another figure lying in the mud. They both claimed they couldn't take another step, and told me to go on and leave them behind as they weren't wounded. But the sight of blood is not the only depressing thing to an aid man. The army calls those who fall out "stragglers" but that's a cruel name. One of these men is 34 and the other is 36. The older one suffers from rheumatism (and that is nothing to be ashamed of where young boys of 19 and 20 suffer the same from living off the ground) and I have been doping him up with aspirins about every night ever since I knew him. I gave them the best pep talk I could but the truth was I had stopped for a breather myself. I grabbed both of their rifles and part of their equipment and we caught up with the platoon again a half hour later. It's a shame to see these older men suffer when there are so many younger men in the rear driving trucks and directing traffic as MP's. Men with war jobs in the states have no argument in regard to age if they are in their 30's, because I have seen too many men in foxholes with graying hair—natural or otherwise.

Will investigate the possibility of a shower now, and will write again after.

SHINJI

P.S. Please send a package of eats!

Mar. 10, 1945

Dear H and E,

Since yesterday our platoon has had showers, change of clothes, saw the Ann Sheridan movie "Animal Kingdom," got our pay, and a good night's sleep indoors. And we can eat our hot chow back here at ease and without nervously gulping it down between artillery shells. That, I believe, has a lot to do with disposition in general.

I received your mail, including the letters of encouragement from Berkeley, and a very nice letter from Bessie. Yep, she seems to have picked out a crusade or two herself along the lines of informing the civilians that there is a war going on. Did she ever tell you of the time she was accosted by some man on the I.C. train for being a Jap? That bum—I wish he could sweat out some of this over here. However, Bessie must have mentioned the incident to me to indicate she has her troubles. I do admit it is a tough situation.

Before I go on please tell Bessie that her cookies are terrific! They really beat anything in the line of pastries that I have had for a long time. Darn, I will write to her to say thanks yet.

Don't worry about those popular songs. Riyo has been asking me what she could send me and what things I wanted to know about, so to make it easier for her to write and still not impose on her too much, I asked her about the latest songs and movies and things like that. Well she was very nice and she began listing all the Hit Parade songs and when we (my friends were in on this too) claimed regretfully that all these song titles were strange to us and that we didn't know any of the songs on the Hit Parade Riyo upped and began sending us the sheet music for the songs. The guys went crazy over the idea and several fellows wanted to write to Riyo and thank her. So that's how we know the music to tunes like "I'm Making Believe," "Till Then," and "I Don't Want to Love You." Riyo sends 'em and Smitty plays 'em. I sure will have to thank her for all these services because we sure appreciate it.

You will have to forgive me if I speak too affectionately of "my" platoon. You just can't help it. The truth is I don't mention them as often as I should, the reason probably being that we hate to talk shop during our hours away from the front lines where life is on borrowed time. Although there are many, many new faces and always new ones to replace the old, probably every aid man in the army thinks of his particular rifle platoon as his own blood and limb. He knows his esteem of them is not partial or prejudiced because he knows the hell they have to go through. And he is not ashamed to admit his "mothering" complex within the platoon because the boys will come to him with their colds, their headaches, or ask him for some pills to stop their GI's (diarrhea), or pills to dope up their coughs before they go out on a combat patrol. They will come to him with all these little ailments and it is not the least disturbing to the aid man because he knows that some day they won't be able to come to him and that he will have to go to them, to try to piece together a hopelessly shattered leg or arm, or maybe to patch a sucking wound in the chest that bubbles every time they breathe, or worst of all to have them die in his arms. As for me, I feel I can't do enough for them on account of all these things. Like the time I was scraping the bottom of my tobacco pouch when some one noticed it and before long the whole company must have known it. "Doc's out of tobacco." "Got any pipe tobacco? The Doc needs some." In an hour I was deluged with pipe tobacco from all over—new packages and old, Prince Albert and Christian Peper, from company supplies to well hidden private supplies in ammo bags to illegitimate pockets in the gas mask. For several days to follow I had to satisfy the query, "Did you get enough tobacco, Doc?" Then there's that embarrasing moment, on pay day when one of the men would come up to me with a fistful of money and say, "Here's your combat pay, Doc, from the boys." That always put a lump in my throat. Things like that convince me that I am with a great bunch of guys. Yep, they don't care about nationality or anything. These boys *are* the front lines, and they are winning the war. I think they are tops.

Well in my enthusiasm I kind of got off the track. I await the first letter from Berkeley which I hope has been written by now. Today being the 10th I am quite sure Eiichi has seen the palm trees in the Sacramento station and has smelled the air from the Pacific.

That's all for now and I await news from California.

SHINJI

P.S. Please send me a package of eats! And if you can buy any film size V616 or PD16 please send it with the camera.

France, 11 Mar. 1945

Dear Mother and Father,

Hello again to all the folks. Am I glad of this chance to write to you again. We are having a short rest right now after some very hard weeks. I hope you didn't mind my not writing because I wrote to Eiichi and Hime at every chance I got and I was counting on them to forward the news to you. I thought of you often and I'm sure that your prayers reached me because sometimes such strange things happened that only someone beyond us could explain. It's hard to write about those things in a letter in words and writing, or to even talk about them, for many times all I could say was only, "Thank God," with the deepest and sincerest gratitude. We will talk about these experiences after the war when I get home. But what I wanted to say was that I *know* your prayers are reaching the right person and that I appreciate it very much. All I can say is that I hope you continue to do so.

Boy but it feels good to be clean again! Yesterday we had our first chance to wash up in about a month. Then we changed into clean clothes and after that we had a real hot meal—roast beef, corn, peas, peaches, bread, and hot coffee. Gee was that good! But best of all we had real night's sleep last night—under a roof. I feel like a new man today. We are waiting now to go see a show they are running for us.

It is March over here but you don't see children playing with kites like back home about this time. Last week it rained and snowed very hard. The wind was cold and it made things very miserable. All our holes filled up with mud and water and it was very hard to keep dry. You would have never recognized me—I was mud from head to toe. I hope it won't be a long time before I can dress and look like the picture on your wall again. The enemy lives in the same kind of mud that we do too, so sometimes it is hard to tell the difference between all the mud-covered soldiers. But don't worry, I'm sure my make-up would frighten any German into wishing that he had never left his sour krauts.

Do you know what I'm thinking about right now. Well, it's about a big plate with a stack of nice hot steaming pancakes with lots of butter and syrup all over them. And beside that is a tall glass of cool white milk. Oh boy, could I go for that right now! Let's see, I haven't seen any fresh milk since leaving the states. And I can also dream about a big chocolate cake with a thick layer of fudge icing on it. Ice cream! Would I go crazy if I could see some ice cream now. And I better stop this before I do go crazy.

You do not have to worry about sending clothes to me because the army takes care of that and they try to get the proper kind to us for this kind of weather. You would be surprised to know what I wear. Would you like to know? Well here goes—on top I have a summer undershirt, T-shirt (from home), winter undershirt, sweat shirt (from home), Red Cross knit sweater, wool shirt, fur lined jacket, combat jacket, and if it rains a raincoat on top of all that. On bottom I have, from inside out, summer shorts, long wool shorts, two wool winter pants, and combat pants. On my feet I wear two cotton socks, two heavy wool long socks, and combat shoes (that leak). Around my neck I wear a G.I. towel for a general purpose scarf and mud wiper. On my head I wear a wool knit cap, a hood (that a German girl sewed for me), and a helmet.

That's some load isn't it? But it still gets cold during those long nights. When I get all my equipment on I look like a ball all rolled up. But all I have to do is to take off all my clothes again to look like a bag of bones again. Don't worry about my weight. All I have to do is to spend a few days of normal living to regain it.

I guess that's all for now. Hope you have heard from Eiichi by now. How is my radio? O.K. I hope because I sure want to hear it when I get home. I hope you won't mind if I listen to some good dance music for one solid month after I get home, because that's what I'm going to do.

I miss all of you very much and am thinking of you all the time.

Your devoted son,

SHINJI

France, 15 Mar. 1945

Dear H and E,

It's a beautiful day—in this Alsace town. Even enough sun to make the Chicago Chamber of Commerce's slogan envious. A bead of sweat actually formed on my forehead today as I plowed through this mud. In our sector all eyes are turned to the sky where there is lots of air activity. Go on, air corps—let's finish this war! Last night just about sunset we had three visitors from the Luftwaffe, and all hell opened up from the ground on these 109's. The orange tracers formed a cone of fire on the unwelcomed visitors. The din was terrific. But I'm afraid the bite was not as effective as the bark—as far as we could see all three got away.

I hope there will be some packages pretty soon. The last four (I got on the same day) were swell but are obviously depleted by now. But that's the way it goes.

Warren got sick to his stomach so they sent him into the clearing hospital. I think he's having trouble with yellow jaundice. And Schubel won a pass to Nancy where he is probably having a good time now on his six cartons of cigs. I hope I get to see Paris after this war—but that's secondary.

Haven't heard anything about that Regimental Citation yet. It must take some time for them to go through, if it goes through. And I hear that in a war where there are so many outfits performing outstanding feats that it is pretty hard to get one.

But today the IG (Inspector General) came down from division with a group of brass hats. They came to see our company in particular—and even more startling, my platoon! Our platoon leader has been up to the CP all day. The platoon runner has been coming back and forth telling the older men to refresh their memories on incidents that took place last December. Gee I wonder what's up.

Speaking of the older men I mean the original bunch. Of that group in this platoon there are only five of us left, including me, that came over with the 44th from Camp Phillips. The rest are all reinforcements. (Who says your prayers didn't work!)

These five consist of my platoon leader (battlefield commission), platoon sergeant, one squad sergeant, one BAR man, and me. And still these new kids come.

Am feeling much better and am in good health. Hope California is treating you O.K. Still waiting for that Berkeley postmark. So long for now,

SHINJI

P.S. Please send a package of eats and some size V616 film if you can get it.

26 Mar. 1945

Dear H and E,

Hello again folks. Hope I didn't cause you to worry for not writing the past few days. Am feeling fine and at present things couldn't be finer. The sun is all out for us and everything is done to the tune of the air corps overhead and to the rumble of motorized movements on the ground. I hope it will end soon in this manner, but knowing the Krauts I know it won't end until the last man quits. But this beautiful sun—it's a life saving sun for the whole damn world.

Not much to make this letter interesting because they say from here on censorship will become even more strict. But I wanted you to know that I'm O.K. and am getting your mail. A little lapse in the packages but I'm sure that when they catch up with us I will have plenty. And don't knock yourself out, Eiichi, in Berkeley because I know you're busy.

Well it was great to see that Berkeley postmark again and to know that Eiichi got there safely. Hoping that you get a good toehold there. Glad to hear about the campus, the Berkeley Music House (thanks for remembering me to Peggy Smith), and that good ol' San Francisco Bay. Almost forget about station KRE, but not quite, so how about letting me know what sort of programs they are putting on, Eiichi.

The boys are fooling around outside with some captured vehicles. Who knows? Maybe we might get to keep one. It's a cheap imitation of a poor man's attempt at a Ford V-8. But when this thing ends it will be something to run around in. There I go optimistically again. I guess it's the sight of the bombers overhead levelling the way for us. Good feeling.

I will write again when I know what the picture is around here. We are rolling—and I mean rolling. But I hope you will be assured by this short note that I am all right.

Eiichi, I enjoyed those "Holland Husks" contrary to your opinion. The closest things to K-ration biscuits are dog biscuits—very hard and dry. We would enjoy salt (white) crackers too. So long for now and good luck in Berkeley. Regards to Walt and Gertrude.

SHINJI

Germany, 1 Apr. 1945

Dear H and E,

Happy Easter to you in Berkeley. I guess you can almost imagine how I am spending mine. I was disappointed to some extent in not being able to spend Easter in one of the famous cathedrals around here. This is certainly the land of cathedrals and some are of classical fame. By that I'm sure you can gather that we are well in Deutschland now. Yes the war has finally come to their doorstep—to be more exact, to their front living room, from where I write now.

It is with a very glad note that I write now because the kind of warfare we are engaged in now is entirely different from those days in the wet holes. I think they call it street cleaning or mopping up in the military. So far the only disagreeable aspects have been the river and canal crossings and the tremendous amount of walking once we are within a city. When we are not walking up one street and then another we ride on tanks tearing up and down the streets as if trying to make as much commotion as possible. We are doing things and seeing people that the average fellow a few years ago never dreamed of. I hope the papers back home mentioned the name of this big town our regiment just took because it was a dilly. The air corps did a beautiful job before us and the proof is right before your eyes. Big outfits like Mercedes-Benz, who didn't make washing machines either, are all flattened out. The civilians of course are still indifferent to us and their thoughts are not for our better health I'm sure. The town still has a telephone system (which played an important part in the town's surrender), running water, street car system, and in many respects it resembles a city back home. All we have to do to get the civilians out of a house is just say that, "Raus!" One thing we can thank the Nazis for is that they thoroughly instilled fear of the uniform into the people so that now when we say *jump* to a German, he jumps! This neighborhood is the better residential district and to us the houses are mansions. The civilians had only about half an hour to clear out. Some day I will send you a picture of our host which I found. He is in civilian clothes now but we have found enough evidence and records in this house to know that he was the head of the Hitlerjugend, or Hitler youth, in this town. Well I must go now, to visit the bathroom, which has modern tiled floors and walls, silvery plated fixtures—and a beautiful flush toilet!

SHINJI

Germany, 2 Apr. 1945

Dear H and E,

A flock of letters from you came yesterday, including a package. I won't bother to mention their dates because they covered February and March pretty well.

All this mail and the fresh eggs we had today are a good sign of the improved transportation behind us. One disagreeable aspect of this rapid advancement has been the tall stacks of K-ration boxes at our supply points. Not exactly inspirational.

I can tell you now where I got that Adolf Hitler Strasse sign. The city was Sarreguemines (or Saargemund in German), quite some time ago. That part of the country took a real beating with some of those towns being taken and then lost and then taken again. This sort of treatment wears a place down. Well Warren finally came back from the hospital to join us again. And he had this to tell me. On his way back to join the outfit he passed through Sarreguemines again and he said that the place is pretty well cleaned up and looking like a thriving big city again. French tricolors all over the place. But most interesting of all was the bit of information that the street corner from which I removed my sign now has a new name—Marshal Foch. Among our other duties it seems that we are renaming streets also.

The war goes on for us from town to town and so far that white flag is always there to greet us. It does not take much imagination to realize that not so long ago swastika flags were draped all over these same places. As for the reasoning behind the white flag, that of course depends on the particular sincerity of the citizens who hang it out. I don't blame them because our tanks are ominous looking and the long stream of troops pouring in should be quite alarming to any do-or-die volksturm. On top of that, our troops enter with trigger fingers in the proper places and with eyes scanning all the windows. Any suspicious movement would call for a tremendous amount of fire (in the case of most G.I.'s "just for the hell of shooting"), and if really serious, one of our tanks would rumble up to the building, point its snout inside the suspicious window and *wham!* one more house is kaput.

I am fine in health and looking hopefully for something to happen this month. But cross your fingers with me.

SHINJI

Germany, 8 April 1945

Dear H and E,

Good news all around. I got your rush letters from Berkeley and I am happy thinking of Mom and Pop being back in Berkeley this very moment. That really was a quick turn of events and you have really and truly convinced me that I will have a swell place to come home to. It's a great feeling.

Thanks for the camera which came in good shape. This $3.98 camera looks strange among the expensive Leicas and Zeiss Ikons that the fellows have recently been acquiring.

When we take a town we usually take the best houses and kick the civilians out on a moment's notice. As tough as it is on the civilians, I try to assume a hardened attitude if not revengeful, because indirectly weren't these very people responsible for all the humiliations and discomforts of yours and Pop's and Mom's and all our friends when they had to suddenly pack up and leave home back in 1942? Since you people faced this predicament once, you would probably be the ones to appreciate the situation here. Sometimes we give the civilians only ten minutes to clear out and you can realize the dither that puts them into. They don't know where to begin, what to take, where to go. They immediately plunge into a scramble and begin to load wagons and baby carriages with the odd unessential things instead of the more useful. They try to take bulky and big furniture with them instead of food or blankets. Calamity could not have a better description. All we can do during this is to glare menacingly for we have been told about teaching them the lesson of the firm hand, this time for good. Now, I am only a Pfc. whose disposition is not toward this strong-arm stuff necessarily, which makes us feel so unnatural and uncomfortable, but it has to be this way. If these Germans think that this is tough, they should have seen what happened in France, not to mention numerous other places that the German army "occupied." Well as I was saying, when these civilians depart so suddenly they forget to take things like guns, cameras, Nazi stuff. We really get them with their pants down—which is good if we figure as the army does, that is, turn it all in. If we don't turn it in but rather we keep it, that's looting, and higher authorities threaten the guilty unit with a bivouac out in the field in pup tents. Which all comes under the heading of modern warfare.

I will see what kind of pictures I can get with the camera. There sure have been several times when I wished that I had one. As for foxholes and slit trenches I don't think we will ever dig another one. They are not particularly pleasant to remember anyway, although it will be hard to convince people back home how miserable and terrible it actually was. No picture could get that.

Incidentally, the fall of Mannheim is Divisional history now (more correctly, Regimental history!) so my platoon Lt. says we can write about it. Enclosed is a copy of "Four by Four," the division rag, which gives an account of it. Of course it fails to mention how we paddled like mad to prevent our assault boat from taking a course similar to a trigonometry professor's nightmare. Oh yes, that lead stuff—German variety—was skipping across the water top too. And yours truly pedaled behind the company on an abandoned bicycle when his feet got too tired of walking up and down the streets of Mannheim during mopping-up proceedings.

Enclosed is also a picture of our "host" in Mannheim who provided us with a fine modern house. I wrote to you from that desk in the picture. He is probably in a P.W. cage now because we found enough evidence to make him/the commandant of the Hitlerjugend in Mannheim. His civilian clothes didn't help. That's what he gets for leaving his picture in his desk. Take it easy,

SHINJI

P.S. Please send a package of eats and some film, size V616 or PD16.

Germany, 14 Apr. 1945

Dear H and E,

Yesterday we learned of our Commander-in-Chief's death and it was hard to believe even though the news that usually gets around to us is reliable. But today we saw it both in writing and in print so that even the wariest of soldiers in a rumor-conscious army is aware of this hard truth. I guess I feel like most G.I.'s in that for a president he was felt intimately among the troops. The average soldier bumps into the wisdom of our former president several times in his army career and is always reassured in his job as a soldier after such contacts. That fact is more so overseas. I remember how relieved I was once after reading a bulletin signed by the President on our status in using gas. He declared that even though we had the upper hand in gas warfare and that even though using gas was just as much a weapon as artillery or bombing, we would not use it offensively "to kill as many Krauts as possible" (as many front line soldiers were inclined to say in particular moments of misery) but that the use of gas was going to be as a retaliatory weapon only. That was going to be the difference between us and them. And now that this thing is almost over we feel as all the people back home must feel now, that it was a shame that he couldn't live to see the end. Speaking for the niseis I guess I don't have to tell you of how grateful we were to both Mrs. Roosevelt and the President.

We are still going easy so may I assure you that you need not worry about me. So long for now. Waiting for mail this week.

SHINJI

P.S. Please send a package of eats and some film, size V616 or PD16, if you can.

Germany, 15 Apr. 1945

Dear H and E,

Sunday morning and believe it or not we are observing it as such. It amounted to an extra hour of sleep this morning and some scrambled eggs for breakfast. There were shells in the eggs so I presume they were fresh although I have known our mess sergeant to put eggshells in his powdered eggs to give the illusion.

The first rumor we awoke to this morning was that one of our armies farther north got into Berlin. This is good to hear although it won't necessarily mean the end of the war (but who knows, by the time you are reading this?). Some G.I. is probably shaking hands with one of Uncle Joe's boys on Unter den Linden. The other rumor this morning insists that our supply sergeant got in a supply of neckties for the company! Shades of garrison life are alarming but its evils are preferred to those screaming mimis and 88's. No mail yet from home this week. So long,

SHINJI

Germany, 15 Apr. 1945

Dear H and E,

At times we almost think that we can figure it out. The country we are passing through is very beautiful. Maybe it's because of the wonderful sun, or maybe it affects us in this manner because of the contrast to the country we just left behind in ruins. Well, on some occasions we get to sit down and meditate—and again I must mention how this sun is very accommodating if not encouraging for this sort of thing. So we light up a pipe or a big not-so-fat cigar (captured of course) and sit on the steps of the particular house we happen to be billeted in, and watch the parade of so-called normal German civilian life pass by. As you may know, all Allied troops occupying Germany are under strict orders against fraternization. Of course the observance of this order becomes more and more difficult with each pair of trim ankles that struts by so flauntingly. A casual "Hi ya, baby!" to some German Judy would cost a fine of some 65 dollars. The fines increase proportionately with the crime and they say death is the penalty for the ultimate of forced intimacy. Well anyway as I was saying, we watch this community going through the duties of spending a day. Most of the villages have been like this one, partly agricultural and mostly self-sufficient, and just quiet on the surface. The tiled roofs and church spires to our eyes are picturesque. The people are much cleaner in Germany than in roofless

France. Their land here has an excellent appearance and, most important to land-minded Germans, there is lots of it. So we begin to figure what a setup all this must have been for the Nazis. A little improvement here and there with lots of flashy hokus-pokus so it will become wedged into the people's mind that the Nazi Party is responsible for all this better living. So, the Party installs flush toilets and a little plumbing here and there. They put out the Volkswagon, the family car, which runs on two cylinders and sends the local citizens into the "new era" hysterics. And the Goering juke box, that's the flashy looking little cabinet radio that every family has (were forced to buy, they say now), which was made in some Goering-owned factory, and which gets only Party stations (as we found out to our curiosity). All this and a flashy army to match. What a deal!

Yesterday we were entertained by Pfc. Mickey Rooney, who is now with a Special Service unit over here. He is a combination of characters as we found out. One of my boys thrust his machine gun into his arms and he was quite willing to pose, so here's hoping the pictures come out. No mail yet this week but not much happening anyway. Am feeling fine.

SHINJI

LETTERS BY TSUCHIDA

Somewhere in Germany, don't know the date

Dear H and E and all the folks,

You would not think that I would be over optimistic about this thing's being a pushover but I guess I was guilty as the next guy in that respect since coming to this sector of Germany. The Seventh Army always seems to pull the tough nuts and although we are going very fast we still have little pockets now and then that give us trouble. Another day and another town. In fact we move so much in one day I lose count of the days and the town. All I can remember nowadays is jumping on tanks and roaring through a town and then walking for endless miles and then another town to shoot up, going up and down the streets with the boys shooting from the hips. These are days full of running and shooting and sometimes ducking a few, smashing doors and windows with the rifle butt and usually thoroughly frightening the civilians. We have been in some beautiful houses today but I never had the chance to sit down long to knock out a letter until now. I saw this typewriter and stationery on this desk so here is my very short letter. Just as I thought, here we go again. Well it was a nice place while it lasted.

Please don't worry about me. I am feeling fine and a good sleep one of these days (maybe) would be all I could ask for. None of my boys have been hit so far for some time now so keep up that praying for us. My only casualties have been the quite venerable members of the Volksturm and the Wehrmacht. Enclosed is their arm band. No letters caught up with us yet. So long for now,

SHINJI

P.S. Please send a package of eats and some film, size V616.

LETTERS BY TSUCHIDA

Austria, 30 Apr. 1945

Dear H and E,

Our above location may be censored but if not that's where we are. We are told that people pay money to see this scenery and to climb these mountains just for the sport. We climb these mountains too and we also pay—with blood sometimes and with tired feet and aching backs, and lots of that cold miserable weather again. The prospects of looking forward to a winter once a year is bad enough but to have it again when it is spring elsewhere is a tough pill to swallow. You know how I hate cold weather. Remind me to steer clear of any place that has snow in the winter after this war.

I got the latest letter with the El Cerrito address. Let me know whether I should convince myself that that is all our own now.

Pop's decision is okay by me although I regret that he can't do anything about his old customers. But how about forgetting the past. I am happy that things turned out the way they did so soon. Thanks to you mostly, Eiichi.

Well we still go on and on and being quite accustomed by now to accepting these far-off places of which I only read and saw pictures of previously with thoughts that I would never see them in my lifetime, we come and leave these historic and scenic spots very casually, our only thoughts being when the hell are we going to stop and sleep.

Yesterday the snow came down again dampening things spiritually and physically. In the morning we had a bright sun that made the all-year-around snow on top of the peaks sparkle. Actually it is very pretty and I curse the war for taking the punch out of the scenic beauty. Normally we would gaze at these beautiful crags and peaks with the snow and mist on top with awe and appreciation of natural beauty, but it's not for us now. How are we going to take that hill? What perfect observation the krauts must have of this whole valley from up there! Ping! Snipers up there. How will I get my casualties down these vertical cliffs? Somebody has to clean these hills out. And we used to brag about our Yosemite Valley in California. Gee whiz, every bend in the road reveals a new and inspiring sight here.

Am writing from a house just as you would picture it—big eaves hang out, rocks on the roof, wide sun balconies outside of the windows. We're billeted on a slope at the foot of another tall peak. Green grass and cows between here and the base. The milkmaid is missing. Some G.I. probably has her cornered already. Have to look straight up from the window to see the top which is mist shrouded. Fir trees begin at the base. That's about it, except for the red and white Austrian flag in place of the swastika of a few days ago.

Well keep up that ol' praying for me. Once you said you wanted to know the truth so here it is (just for you though, Eiichi). We got pinned down again yesterday in the hills and I'm afraid I had to practice my profession on some of my boys. I have a straight edge razor that I keep in my aid kit that I use for cutting clothes away quick and yesterday I was using it while cutting off a guy's clothes and ping! It shot right out of my hand a couple of inches from my nose. It doesn't bother me any more because close ones like that, that take buttons off sometimes, are so frequent. Just figure that when you get it you get it and just hope that it isn't too bad (the unwritten creed in the infantry, incidentally). After that I just pulled my head down a little lower and kept on working. But the lousy part is that somebody behind me got mine, but not bad. Well here we go again. So long for now and keep writing.

SHINJI

You know where, 4 May '45

Dear H and E,

I just realized that we are not supposed to tell you where we are but few days ago I did so you should know. In case you don't, we are way up here and I mean way up here in the snow. I've seen it all but the yodeling and if I can help it I don't want to stick around here just for that. My nerves are just about back to normal again and I guess it wouldn't hurt to kind of reminisce over the events of the last few days.

It's a great feeling to see all the armor and trucks and guns and men rolling down this pass now. Vehicles of every description, engineer equipment and bulldozers are going one way and truck loads of German prisoners going the other. We are kind of taking a breather now and I guess we deserve it because a few days ago this sight wasn't in existence. I don't know what the definitions for a hero are but I can easily say that I have known and lived with them. You probably won't read about some obscure privates and sergeants giving their lives to hasten the opening of this pass in the papers. Probably even the drivers who tear down this slope now so easily don't realize what it cost us to take it.

But the men in this company will never forget these mountains and what it meant to knock off another day of this war in this sector in the deeds of a few guys that we used to know. And to think that a few weeks ago we were damned sure about never sweating it out again. That's what makes it hurt more than ever now that it's almost all over.

We started up the pass and got sniped at all the way. It was perfect terrain—for the krauts. I don't recall seeing any in all that time. There was one roadblock after the other and man-made landslides conveniently placed at precipitous spots. These spots were zeroed in so that anybody who faltered at these barriers got picked off. The armor couldn't get over these ticklish spots so it was strictly us by ourselves. We left the road and took off up the mountains and unless you are a mountain goat, that is no fun. One after another they picked us off and you never knew when you were going to get one too. All of you folks must have been praying on May 1st because I know of no other explanations for being spared. Even as I worked on one of my friends they kept on shooting. I even tried waving a piece of white bandage and that didn't seem to do any good because *ping!* another one went into the body of my friend and that finished him. It went right between my knees.

After that they knew we were in the woods so they pasted us with direct-fire artillery. Our artillery couldn't help because of these mountains, and anyway they reminded us of anti-aircraft guns the way they were pointed straight up. This was face to face stuff and that kind of eliminates the use of our artillery because they fire at some coördinates on a map and I doubt if unseen snipers can be located by map coördinates. We finally got to the top of the pass where another roadblock and a whole garrison of Germans waited for us with everything in the books. They told us later that they were remnants of SS officers determined to fight to the end.

They must have saved up some ammunition of every description for this stand because when the platoon rushed in literally everything opened up—machine guns, burp guns, bazookas, rockets, anti-tank grenades, hand grenades, and an 88 anti-aircraft gun was parked at the end of the street with its muzzle pointed down the street firing point-blank. I expected any minute to be cut off from the rear and be surrounded. We rushed the end building and used it for a miniature fortress. This was possible only because a few of the boys held them off. One of my friends kept firing his BAR from the shoulder and when he was hit he continued shooting from his knees. He was hit again but he kept firing until he fell over dead beside the building. Another boy was hit in the stomach and he crawled over to a hole. Me, I should have gone to him but I just couldn't. He kept telling me to stay where I was and not to bother over him. Instead he sat up and calmly held a pistol in his lap and kept shooting, until a few more slugs entered him. I can still see him, and I guess I always will, yelling to me, "Keep down, Willie, don't come over!" Now do you know what I mean about heroes? And I guess you can see why I don't give a hoot about medals or ratings.

It's knowing and living side by side with boys like these that kind of makes medals and rating infinitesimally unimportant.

Fortunately this building we took was concrete and it withstood all the rockets that they threw at us. The building next door, a tourist lodge in pre-war times, was partly wooden so the Germans set it on fire with some sort of gasoline concoction. The fire made the night seem like day and we must have made a wonderful target. By morning we were relieved and I guess we had done our job well, but the sight of our buddies crumpled up in the snow and scattered around by the building still holding their guns, and the anxiety of wondering the fate of our friends who were captured during this stand, makes us wish that everybody could know the cost of winning this war. So as we sit here today in one of the houses at the other end of the pass, watching all the vehicles roll by, we wonder if we couldn't rename this pass after one of our boys just as long as some G.I. is using it. Once again our platoon has dwindled but I know it took a lot of Heinies to do it.

Will get some good sleep now. Even have a bed picked out and here I go. Am feeling O.K. Thanks for the card to send Mom. So long for now,　　Shinji

Any day now!

Still here, 6 May 1945

Dear H and E,

Just a line to let you know that things are tops over here now. The outfit that relieved us the other day kept going until they met up with the boys from Italy. Our job here is done. I'm so darn happy about it. All I have to do now is hear somebody say it's over, and I expect that any time. But nobody has to tell us really, because we know and feel it.

All the Nazi big shots who tried to get away ran into the 5th Army if they went south. I hope you read about how Von Kesselring gave up to our 44th Div. CO, General Dean. This happened the other day.

Oh boy it's good. I think I'll sit here and soak up this thing called peace for a while. The Pacific deal isn't going to bother me at present. Nothing will. I will cross my bridges as I get to them.

We couldn't have come to a better place for this rest. I can't tell you where I am but I couldn't use the adjective alpine to a better advantage than at present. It just goes to show basically that natural beauty appeals to most of us. Only a few days ago the same kind of terrain was full of the worst kind of man-made hell and terror. Some of my boys haven't even had the chance to wash off the powder burns from their clothes yet. But darn if here we aren't just up to our necks in alpine beauty and liking it. We are in the prettiest little town you ever saw. It's down in the valley between a couple of snow-capped ridges and all the likely ingredients have been included in this backdrop. Right smack outside of my window balcony is a waterfall. Beneath that is a 100% honest-to-God mountain stream if I ever saw one. The water is so clear you could spot a coin in it a mile away. Hold it a second.—— H and E, this is good! Two "ghosts" just walked in the room to see me, two friends of mine that I and all the rest of the platoon had given up for dead so long ago. They had been prisoners of the Germans near here and when the Americans came in they were abandoned. Oh gee whiz but everything is right and good tonight! I will write later. Thanks for praying, honest.

SHINJI

9 May 1945

Dear Folks,

It's really over now and I know you are rejoicing with me. Lots to say so here goes. First of all here's the picture as we see it now.

We took over a tourist's hotel for our billet and I guess you can call what we are doing occupational service in a belligerent country. I have enclosed a picture postcard of the place and the town that we are in. You can see the wonderful background. I didn't bother to cut the name of the town off the picture so here's hoping you get it. Nuts to it. It's the sweetest little place you ever saw, the perfect place to recuperate from 88's and hand grenades and screaming mimis! All the men have a bed and homey-like rooms. Electricity, bed lamps, basins with running water in all the rooms, and as I write this my mood is set by the music of Duke Ellington. Yep, a radio. Step out on the balcony and take a sun bath on the reclining chair. The first floor is the dining room and kitchen, so taking advantage of natural assets, our mess sergeant set up his stoves in there and we eat off of plates if we like. But it's so nice outside that most of us eat at the tables underneath those trees you see in the picture. And there is a tap room for the boys—beer out of these beautiful porcelain mugs. These mugs fascinate me more than the beer.

I'll have to tell you about my personal valet, my runner so to speak. The first day we were here I fixed his hands up where they were cut pretty badly and ever since he has been hanging around wanting to do things for me so we kind of got attached to each other. He is a kid about 9 or 10 and his name is Heinrich but I told him from now on it was going to be Henry. I give him some candy now and then and let him eat some of our chow and for this he runs around all day for me. You see I sleep in the room with the platoon Lt. and the platoon Sgt., so as far as he is concerned, we are all generals to him. And his sister fits into this too. She is very attractive, unmarried but has that one inevitable child of a German soldier. Now before you get me wrong, Henry has his mother and sister providing and changing the sheets on our beds, and our clothes have been washed and ironed several times now through the efforts of Henry's management.

This place is spacious enough to afford me one room to use as an aid station. This is all in the spirit of the place and the moment, of course, because the battalion is the smallest unit to have an aid station. Somebody suggested upon finding one particularly white walled room, "Hey, doc, why don't you put your stuff in here for an aid station?" and I did. Henry got some white sheets from his mother and we draped one over a table. I emptied the contents of my aid kits on the table and lined up all my dressings and bottles and scissors in a professional manner. But before Henry could accuse me of unsterile technique I had to brush the mud of the battlefield off of much of the dressings and equipment.

He was much impressed by my bloodstained scissors. "Deutscher soldat," I told him to scare him. Incidentally, he carted all the trash in this room up to the attic. I have my captured red-cross flag tacked on the door and one of the boys wrote "Doc Willy" on a genuine piece of shingle which now hangs correctly on the door. Boy I get a kick out of this. And oh the customers that I get! Oo-la-la! Now get this, it will send you. *I*, who happen to be the aid man with this company occupying this town, am the town's only representative of the medical profession. So what happens but the civilians come here too! They don't know it, but aspirins are plenty cheap and I prescribe them for a cure-all. Especially when these pretty girls come, the guys have a grand time calling me Herr Doctor or Herr Hauptmann and they really believe I am. I enjoy it but I also dread the moment when I may have to deliver a baby or something! And God bless the naïveté of the girls in this hyar part of the country—wow! If they only knew how crimson I get underneath this oriental "tan."

I'd better sign off now. Will continue tomorrow. Please send no more candles. We've got electricity, and if not I'll "liberate" candles. Plenty of tobacco now so that's enough. So long,

SHINJI

Same place, 9 May 1945

Dear Eiichi,

A separate letter to you first of all to let you know that you may use my bonds any time in any way you please. Let me know if you have been getting two 25-dollar bonds (i.e., a $37.50 bond) a month as I have been paying for them since coming overseas. And forget about paying it back. What you have been doing taking care of the family is beyond my paying in mere dough.

The allotment for ma is started to be investigated tonight. The company furnished me a jeep to ride all the way to the town where Regiment is today and in a few days I will send you the blanks to be filled in. When you send them back they will again be investigated. So expect about a month for it to be decided.

Also had all my records changed to the new address—that in El Cerrito.

Eiichi, let me know who you want me to put the pressure on. My chaplain, my platoon Lt., and best of all every man left in my platoon will back me up. These Pennsylvania Irish are tough birds, and true as arrows.

Also, I got a Bronze Star for our deal on New Years. I told you, I think, of how it was on Jan. 1. The citation was very flattering and they gave me a mimeographed copy of it, but it is restricted so I will bring home the copy with me. That's the way they work these Bronze Stars. You get just a ribbon now. The medal and bull comes after the war, which is now, so maybe one of these days I will see what the thing looks like.

This is also strictly confidential but via the grapevine. My friend who is the company clerk told me that a Silver has been put in for me. They are hard to get, and among men who are each and every one unrecognized and unpraised individual heroes, I feel hardly worthy of the award, or even being mentioned for one.

Oh yes, while we're at it I have a cluster to my Purple Heart now because I got hit in my right wrist this time (by a Panzerfaust fragment). Two pieces. I am always lucky as I always get the small ones. That makes a total of 6 holes in me, all small. No, I didn't have to be evacuated. After all what good is a medic if he can't treat himself.

You take it easy, too.

SHINJI

LETTERS BY TSUCHIDA

Tauberbischofsheim, Germany, June 9, 1945

Dear H and E and Mom and Papa and All,

Hello again folks. Yes, we are back in Germany again and by the name of this town you would think that the size of the town would be in proportion to the length of the name. But it isn't a very big place. A few farms and mostly pasture land. I think the closest big city is Stuttgart and that I am sure you have heard of. In our fight across Germany we paved the way almost to Stuttgart when the Free French came through us and took the city proper and also the credit for that city.

I still do not know our fate. We are living out in the fields again in pup tents lined up in orderly fashion. I believe we as individuals are undergoing a screening process of some sort. It appears that we are waiting and waiting.

I now look back on my stay in Austria as one of the most pleasant five weeks of my life. Those beautiful Tyrolian Alps. They really grew on us. Right now we are in a flatter part of Germany and I miss the presence of those beautiful peaks around and above us as we had in Austria. I envy those who will stay there as occupational troops. Beautiful country, beautiful weather, and beautiful girls. It was too good. I remember how we cursed those mountains the first week in May because it was such hard fighting. And I also remember saying, how can people pay good money to see this? Now that the element of death and fighting has been removed it makes all the difference in the world as you may suspect. Basically and inwardly we should hate and dread the sight of these mountains because we lost so many friends here and living was so miserably hard. But it doesn't work out that way. *Even* the infantry soldier is subject to yielding to natural beauty although terrain was a matter of life and death to him only a short while ago.

This typewriter is from the last place we were in Austria. We are going to try to keep it in the platoon as long as possible. Bye,

SHINJI

LETTERS BY TSUCHIDA

Tauberbischofsheim, Germany, 10 June 1945

Dear H and E,

The mail is getting a little faster from home with your letter of the first of June here. Am sitting out in front of our pup tent tonight since it's not raining, so I will knock out a fast one. I still say it's a wonderful feeling to know that I will be alive tomorrow morning, and that the nights will not be so horrible any more. I don't relish this sleeping on the ground any at all. One wakes up in the morning feeling the dampness all the way to the bones, and the dew is all over your blankets. All my bones still ache pretty badly and I think it will take a couple of years to sweat it out of my system completely. Comparatively speaking, it's still a luxury to be able to take your shoes off at night.

Morale here is fine if not tops for the reasons stated above. But the biggest factor is that everybody thinks we are going home. By the way we talk we are half way home now. Boy just wait till the 44th—New York's own 44th—marches down Fifth Avenue, they are saying. I can assure you that we have had lots of experience in taking over a town and if we ever hit N. Y. as a unit—wow! We talk of sending scouts out, then a patrol with flank security, in taking N. Y. We'll shoot the place up with burp guns and BAR's and if they won't let us into a certain place we'll shoot the door down. That's the way we are talking now.

There's one boy here who says I shouldn't live in California. His name is Paul Shaw and he insists that he is going to take me to his home town in Texas to live. In fact I have had several offers. Thomas McCarthy says that I am going to finish my college at Syracuse, New York, and live with him in Fulton. Then there's the old man of the platoon, Louis Scavo. He's Italian and he insists that I live with him in Pennsylvania. He says, "Why my wife would feed you so much 'guinea' food that you would never want to leave." All these boys say these things with sincerity and I know their sincerity. What do you think of all this? They make it sound so good sometimes that I am almost inclined to take them up on it.

I don't think I ever described the Leica to you yet. It has an f2. lens and 1/500th to 1 second shutter. Range finder on it, of course. I also have the light meter to go with it and since it was built especially for the Leica all the stops correspond with the camera. Gee, I wish I had some film for it. Wish me luck on getting it home. Also my Luger pistol.

In closing I want to say that the boys just finished a big crap game. McCarthy just ran over to me to show me his big roll of Marks. "Don't think I'm bad for gambling with my own boys, Willy," he says, "because this is for the fund." "What fund?" I ask him. "Why, the Have-Fun-in-New York Fund," he says. He is going to see that every man in the platoon is going to have a good time on his winnings. Well, anyway we are very optimistic about it all.

Getting dark now. So long,   SHINJI

Please send a package of eats and some 35mm film if you can get it.

Germany, 14 June 1945

Dear H and E,

I am happy to announce that this is going to be my last letter from Germany and possibly from Europe. I am definitely coming home for a recuperation period that may last from 21 to 30 days. After that the division as a unit will train for the Pacific. Whether I will stay with them or not, I do not know. And when we will leave for the States I do not know, or the place where we will land. We are undergoing processes just in reverse to that of leaving the States. It is a little symbolic to us when we turn in our equipment, and not just getting a damn load off of our backs. Gas masks, for instance, used to carry all our treasured extra junk, and the shovel carved so many of our homes. I used to hate my steel helmet but now I realize that home for the last seven months or so has been underneath that helmet. It may be hard for you to understand, but I believe I have become quite attached to it.

In the past few weeks we have been experiencing rare coincidences in retracing the route we took in our advance across Germany. The sight of an old battle site had many effects on us. We would be driving along on the trucks when all of a sudden we would come across a certain area where the fighting was particularly hard. In places like that we knew every tree, every rock, every knoll, every bush by heart (and probably will for the rest of our lives). So we would all stand up and begin to talk excitedly, pointing to the different objects and then remarking on the incidents associated with them. "That's where I got two krauts!" and "That's the tree the dud hit," and some of the wounded fellows who have come back to rejoin the outfit remembered exactly the spot they were hit. And, many of our hastily dug foxholes and slit trenches still remain unfilled. I saw one of mine by the road just as I left it, still as full of mud and water as ever. In other places where the farmers were particularly progressive they have filled in our holes and those of gun emplacements and have begun to plant and plow over them. Inevitably we often drove by the places where we lost many of our good friends. At those places the boys were quiet and someone would just say, "That's Schwartzi's place" or "That's where Rossi got it." Somebody else would curse the Germans. I always felt like saluting those spots but somehow I never did. It's beyond that. We also came across buildings that were landmarks to us, too. Once we were fighting from a house and the Germans were throwing everything at that building. Finally they used white phosphorus shells which set the house on fire. We had a cellar full of both German and American soldiers sweating out the shelling. The Germans were our prisoners and altogether there must have been about twenty of them along with about five civilian women and two old men. When the place began to burn down we had to leave it in quick dashes because the Germans were using MG's on all the doorways and windows. As we drove by that building about a week ago we saw that it had burned to the ground. I almost wanted to stop to see if the prisoners got out. And then there were some of the woods which we went by, reminding us of the ordeal we went through in occupying and clearing them out. The sight of those woods was like a repeating nightmare and I just shuddered.

Where it was possible I took pictures of these places and I hope they come out. I will have lots of films to develop when I get home.

Last night for chow we had some rice, which in the army is invariably prepared as rice pudding, but last night the cooks made it steamed rice. Did the guys howl about that. They're poisoning our minds as well as our stomachs for the CBI!! Secretly, I kind of liked it because it reminded me a little of mama's cooking. Boy, I can't wait to get home and really eat!!!!! I hope you can buy chocolate cakes and ice cream in El Cerrito.

Yes, Eiichi, you are right. The means of livelihood is my biggest concern because I don't know a thing and can't do a thing specifically. I sure hope your optometry shop shapes up right. Maybe it's still not too late to finish engineering.

I had planned to send you and Hime a cablegram just a few days before your second wedding anniversary, but we may be in a place where that is impossible when that time comes so I would like to now wish you and Hime continued happiness in your marriage. I could not have had a better "home front" team than you two. Now that the time has come when I can almost see my boat ride home I want you to really know that your letters, thoughts, and sympathies helped to pull me through with a fair resemblance of a sane and appreciative mind. And also thanks for the countless number of packages, which I still claim to be the best in the outfit. Not a single "casualty" among the packages which are now familiar to possibly every appreciative mail-clerk down the line.

Please keep writing and sending, however, as before. So long and I'LL BE SEEING YOU SOON.   SHINJI

P.S. Please send a package of eats and some 35mm film.

Rheims, France, 26 June 1945

Dear H and E,

Today I left a part of me behind—just as much a part of me as my right arm. Yes, I mean the Second Platoon of I Company. Gee, it was awful to find out that I was going to be left behind here in France and the outfit going home. I hope you won't be too disappointed because I must ask you to be a little patient for a few more months before I can come home. Here is what happened. Yamate and I and another nisei in the division and all the above-85-points men, and all the class D men are going to be left behind in order to make room for all the Pacific bound G.I.'s who have highest priority to the States. We will stay here until they have boat space for us.

Please forgive me for not writing too much now but doggone it I feel awful about leaving the boys. I shook hands with all the men and gee it got worse as I went down the line. Well, we had to part sometime but I wish it wasn't like this. I guess I cried a little bit but so did my good friends. Hell, I wish I could trade my right arm to go home with them. Will write again later. Your letters are coming fine.

SHINJI

Mourmelon, France, 22 July 1945

Dear Folks,

Don't be alarmed at the new address but it looks as if I wound up in the hospital—as a patient. My back ached and my legs hurt so they gave me a general check-up all over. They are not going to do anything about my back but when they got to my legs they took about 9 X-rays. They want me to take it easy and declared me to be in Class 4-D, which is equivalent to the civilian 4-F. That also makes me ZI, or in military terminology, zone of interior, which is another way of spelling U.S.A. So for all I know ZI's have a very good chance of coming home. Emergency ZI cases are even flown home in C-47's but I will be thankful for even a boat ride. Except for the aches in all my joints from head to toe, a nice souvenir from last winter, I am all right. Figure it as a break for me because now I am living in clean pajamas, sleeping in sheets, and the shower facilities are a luxury.

Did you get a sketch of me done in pencil from Brussels yet? I forgot the man's name but he did it for me for a pack of cigarettes. You may wonder what I'm doing with the Combat Infantryman Badge. My platoon gave that to me just before I left and boy I wouldn't part with that for anything. They told me to wear it proudly. If anybody challenges it, I'm to notify the entire platoon.

Good-by for now, SHINJI

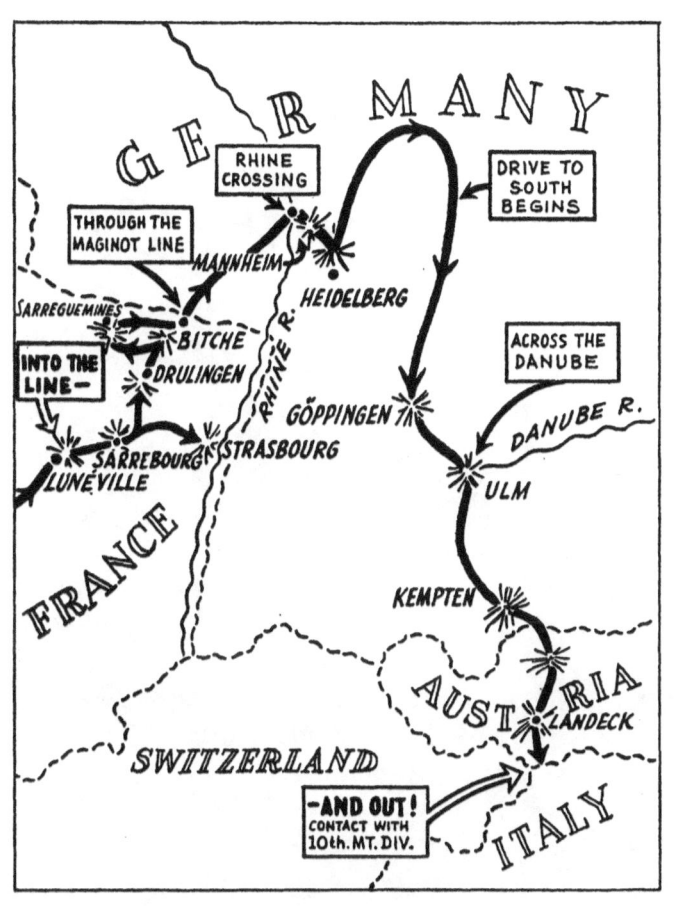

THE 44TH'S ROUTE AND BATTLES

www.ingramcontent.com/pod-product-compliance
Lightning Source LLC
Chambersburg PA
CBHW021711230426
43668CB00008B/804